START LIVING THE GOOD LIFE—
IT WILL COST YOU NOTHING AT ALL!

Madison Avenue's latest gimmick is "the good life." We are told if we will buy this home, try this product, move to this community, join this club, or serve this whiskey, we will begin to enjoy "the good life." But the promises are empty.

The Bible declares that "the good life" is something money can't buy. The really good life is enjoyed by people who are morally and spiritually disciplined. God's way to the good life is no secret. He has shown us ten steps to good living in the ageless Ten Commandments. Here is His way to the good life.

—ROBERT H. SCHULLER

GOD'S WAY TO THE GOOD LIFE

ROBERT H. SCHULLER

BANTAM BOOKS
TORONTO · NEW YORK · LONDON · SYDNEY · AUCKLAND

*This low-priced Bantam Book
has been completely reset in a type face
designed for easy reading, and was printed
from new plates. It contains the complete
text of the original hard-cover edition.*
NOT ONE WORD HAS BEEN OMITTED.

GOD'S WAY TO THE GOOD LIFE

*A Bantam Book / published by arrangement with
Keats Publishing Company*

PRINTING HISTORY

*Keats edition published in 1974
Bantam edition / October 1987*

*The article "The Glass Cathedral That Grew in an Orange
Grove" by Lois Joice, originally appeared in* The Church
Herald, *April 16, 1971, and is reprinted with permission.* The
Church Herald *is the official magazine of the Reformed
Church in America.*

ISBN 0-553-26803-1

Published simultaneously in the United States and Canada

*Bantam Books are published by Bantam Books, Inc. Its trade-
mark, consisting of the words "Bantam Books" and the por-
trayal of a rooster, is Registered in U.S. Patent and Trademark
Office and in other countries. Marca Registrada, Bantam
Books, Inc., 666 Fifth Avenue, New York, New York 10103.*

PRINTED IN THE UNITED STATES OF AMERICA

O   0 9 8 7 6 5 4 3 2 1

*Affectionately dedicated to my father
Anthony Schuller and my mother
Jennie Beltman Schuller who first taught me
God's Way to the Good Life*

CONTENTS

FOREWORD

By Norman Vincent Peale

A preacher whose faith is firmly based on the Bible and completely Christ-centered, and who also has the ability to communicate the Gospel to the teeming population of a huge urban complex is admirable indeed. And if this preacher also brings to the Christian ministry a promotional and administrative capacity usually reserved to business executives and combines this with a humble loving service to his Lord his contribution to the Kingdom is considerable.

Robert Schuller, author of this volume, is a preacher and pastor who may be described in these terms. I knew him first when he was sent by the Board of Domestic Missions into sprawling, booming Orange County, California, to establish a church. For this area, said to be having the most phenomenal growth of any county in the United States, our Board with true Christian statesmanship selected a man who combined thorough Christian dedication with the energy and resourcefulness required to bring Christ to those multitudes.

In 1955 he arrived and immediately arranged for services in a drive-in theater. Any thought that such an unusual procedure might be lacking in reverence and dignity was entirely dissipated by a visit to these unique services. I had the privilege of preaching for him to several thousand people seated in their cars, and was deeply moved by the large cross which had been erected and the sweet old hymn music that filled the air. I shall never forget Mr. Schuller saying to the worshiping multitude: "Only Christ is honored here . . . our Saviour who shed His blood on this cross for our salvation." That humble, strong statement communicated a depth of sincerity that soon made itself felt, and people were won to the Master.

Gradually a strong true church evolved. It was my joyful experience to preach at the dedication of a beautiful sanctuary seven years after those humble beginnings, and I had no doubt at all that the Garden Grove Community Church is the house of God and of His Son, Jesus Christ.

This book is a succinct and extraordinarily well-written statement of a vital Christian message. In terse sentences that bristle with life, the author puts the Gospel straight up against the paganism of our time. He speaks in the thought and language forms that are understandable to the people of our day and generation. There is no uncertain note; it is the Gospel of Jesus straight out of the New Testament and it is beamed to the mind and heart with consummate effectiveness.

To a generation that has not been taught the good life with the oldtime certainty and so has often lost its way, Mr. Schuller points clearly down the straight road to the Cross of Christ.

This is an appealing book and there is spiritual power in it. It has a manly quality and the sturdy faith it expresses is good for the soul.

—NORMAN VINCENT PEALE

PREFACE

Madison Avenue's latest gimmick is "the good life." You know what I mean. We are told if we will buy this home, try this product, move to this community, join this club, or serve this whiskey, we will begin to enjoy "the good life."

Now the appeal is legitimate. But the promises are empty. We are being brainwashed into believing that the good life is something you can buy. Of course this is not true.

Americans have more gadgets, appliances, trinkets and things than any other people on the face of this earth. We are the richest nation in the world.

Yet we have more trouble with anxieties, worries, and fears, to say nothing of boredom, than perhaps any other nation. What's wrong?

Well, with unflinching intensity, the Bible declares that "the good life" is something money can't buy. The really good life is enjoyed by people who are morally and spiritually disciplined. God's way to the good life is no secret. He has shown us ten steps to good living in the ageless Ten Commandments. Here is His way to the good life.

—ROBERT SCHULLER

Garden Grove, California

ACKNOWLEDGMENTS

Achievement is seldom possible in isolation.

And if the publication of this slim volume is by any standard an accomplishment, then credit must go first to the many writers, lecturers, and teachers who have stimulated me and supplied material through my years of study. To identify them at this point would be like taking a cup of water from the gulf and giving credit to the right river!

The great congregation of the Garden Grove Community Church has been steady as the north star in supplying me with inspiration. In this church I have always been encouraged to dream great dreams, and been given enough liberty in leadership to direct these dreams to fulfillment. This book is only a single illustration. It is this congregation that insisted that this material, first presented in sermon form, be prepared for wider distribution.

Now let me salute my faithful secretaries Betty Nebel and Lois Wendell for first preparing these chapters for publication, and finally Ruth Bostick and Carol DeYoung for typing the completed manuscript.

I am profoundly grateful to my very good friend Norman Vincent Peale, who took time to read this manuscript and offer inspiring encouragement.

—R.S.

INTRODUCTION

The Glass Cathedral
That Grew In an Orange Grove

By Lois M. Joice

The weather was miserable, the sort of bone-chilling drizzle that keeps Southern Californians home from church in droves. A perfect day to go back to sleep or curl up with a book; yet throughout the day, I saw thousands of radiant Christians streaming in and out of Garden Grove Community Church, and thousands more worshiping in the drive-in facility.

We hear that the institutional church is losing its appeal, that it is failing to win new followers for Christ, or even to hold its own people. But if this is true, how do you explain Garden Grove?

There are some things you won't find in this church. No emphasis on guilt and self-abasement, for example. What you *will* find is an atmosphere of victorious, confident Christianity which says more clearly than words could say, "With God all things are possible."

Theologians might argue the pros and cons of this approach. What no one can dispute, however, is that *something is happening there*. The church is gloriously alive, reaching the normally unreachable and restructuring lives. Whatever they are doing at Garden Grove, it is working.

The church has been called the "great glass

cathedral that rose up among the orange groves," and is widely known as the world's first walk-in, drive-in worship center.

Most of the credit goes to the founding pastor, Robert Schuller. He had the vision that created this incredible reality. Oldtimers point to the nearby Orange Drive-in Theatre and tell how the whole thing started there, in 1955 with Bob Schuller preaching from the snack-bar roof to a handful of cars.

Today, from a balcony pulpit beside a massive, sliding glass door, he speaks simultaneously to overflow congregations within the sanctuary and out in the drive-in, and to the largest congregation of all, the television audience. Since 1970, the entire Garden Grove morning service has been shown live in countless Southern California homes.

"God always provides if we think big and believe big," Mr. Schuller will tell you. Known as the "possibility-thinking pastor," he is not greatly surprised by the phenomenal growth of the church he built. After all, with God all things are possible.

"Possibility thinkers don't quit when they are faced with a mountain," he says. "They keep on striving until they climb over, find a pass through, tunnel underneath—or simply stay and turn their mountain into a gold mine."

The church is a masterpiece and could take its place among the great European sanctuaries which were erected to the glory of God and have fed the souls of men for generations. The sanctuary and its setting are designed to express the serenity of the Twenty-third Psalm. Twelve fountains, symbolizing the Apostles, bubble up from the quiet waters of a block-long reflection pool. Green pastures, lush lawns, crystal buildings, and a life-sized gold-leaf statue of the Good Shepherd all contribute to the peaceful mood.

The essence of Garden Grove is not to be found in buildings and gardens, however dramatically beautiful, but in the people who worship there. One quickly senses that these people are working together, supporting one another in the struggle to live fully the new life in Christ. In the small talk-it-over groups which have become such a dynamic force, members frequently ask each other: How did you and God get along last week? Did you put in a good word for Jesus Christ? Did you love another person at *his* point of need?

Determined that Garden Grove will not be thought of as "Schuller's Church," the senior pastor has built a team of thirteen competent men and women. Each staff member is a vital part of the total ministry, and each approaches his responsibilities with a spirit of excitement and enthusiasm that makes Christianity a living force. Kenneth Van Wyk, for example, youthful and dynamic Minister of Education, who has built the Sunday school to its present membership of 3,000, and Harold Leetsma, warm, loving, and filled with the confidence born of complete faith. He is an excellent Minister of Evangelism.

"The secret of this church is that every member thinks of himself as a missionary," says Mr. Leetsma. "Most members came originally at another member's urging." Harold Leetsma's special workers are the Shepherds, a force of several hundred men he has trained to make contact with the host of unchurched of Orange County.

More than 65 percent of those who join the church are new Christians. Mr. Leetsma conducts the seven-week pastor's classes, which are required of all new members, instructing several hundred families each year. He reaches out in love to each individual, and wants to establish a real relationship with all of them.

"So many wonderful stories have come out of this church," he says. "We are always hearing about people who have been alone in a motel and ready to end it all when they looked up and saw our lighted cross high in the sky."

The tall Tower of Hope, topped by a slim, contemporary cross visible for miles, has become a symbol of the church's concern for people who need help. "People caring for people" is how members see their mission, and they spend many thousands of hours in voluntary service to others.

Human problems are consciously sought out and attacked at the point of greatest need. There is a desire to fill the hunger for God that they see in the eyes of their neighbors.

"We believe so much in what is happening here that we want to share it with everyone," says Dorothy Herrin. She and her husband, Wade, attended another church for years, but were "getting nothing from it." Now they are both involved in various ways at Garden Grove. "The church is the center of our lives now, and we have become different people," Wade comments. "We feel Christ's spirit is here in this congregation."

A dramatic manifestation of the church's philosophy of concern is the Dial New Hope telephone counseling project, directed by Dr. Raymond Beckering, Minister of Family and Parish Life.

From a modest room high in the Tower of Hope, a life line goes out to the community around the clock, dedicated to "giving new hope when all other hope seems to fail."

What sort of people dial New Hope? Alcoholics, unwed mothers, the lonely, the aged, young people with a drug problem, and potential suicides. Some weeks, a suicide a day has been prevented. Dr. Beckering says, "If we had saved only one person, our work would have been worthwhile."

The 350 lay volunteers who man the lines in four-hour shifts have available a complete listing of community resources. But problems are not automatically referred to other agencies.

"Referral can be an easy way out," Dr. Beckering says. "We train our people to resolve the problem on the spot if possible. We also train them not to give pat answers like "Pray," or "Have faith.""

What the caller can expect is counsel with compassion, not censure, and without the jargon of the professional. If the situation warrants it, callers are invited to come to the Tower of Hope for further guidance, without cost, from Dr. Beckering and his specially trained staff of counselors.

Garden Grove Church continues to grow at an astonishing pace, but Bob Schuller is less interested in numbers than in the quality of his flock's spiritual life.

"What does God want us to do that we are not yet doing? How will he use the things that are happening here? You know," he muses, "I have an idea that our greatest opportunities and our greatest contributions are still ahead of us here at Garden Grove. Who knows what God will call us to do next?"

When a pastor and a congregation are led by God and a belief in possibility thinking, who indeed can say what great new challenge will come next?

GOD'S WAY
TO
THE GOOD LIFE

PART I: GET RELIGION

1. Choose the Right God
2. Find Out What God is Really Like
3. Then Take God Seriously
4. And Keep in Constant Touch With Him

The First Commandment:
"Thou shalt have no other gods before me"

The first commandment points us to the good life by reminding us that we can overcome our insecurity if we will follow the Saviour's God—the God who gave these Ten Commandments, the invisible One who flung burning stars, searing suns, and spinning satellites soaring through space: who in the misty dawn of creation breathed into a glorified mass of dust the human spirit. This all-powerful, all-knowing, all-wise, everywhere-present God is the God that Jesus worshiped. If the first commandment says anything to us today it is this: O quivering, frightened world, behold and believe in the God of the Christ! The Saviour's God is the only source of inner security!

Chapter One

CHOOSE THE RIGHT GOD

The real problem of our time is an old problem:
We worship the wrong god.

Man has always had a wide variety of gods. Bacchus, the ancient Greek god of wine, has his devotees to this day. Venus, the goddess of love, is wildly revived in our sex-obsessed world of the twentieth century. Athena, the goddess of wisdom, has once more been elevated to glory. For we see an almost blind assent by the masses to any lofty pronouncements that come from "intellectual quar-

ters." Meanwhile the Eternal waits in merciful pa-
tience for the world to discover Him once more in
His Word.

Who is your god? Everybody has a god. We are
instinctively and incurably religious. This explains
man's universal insecurity. Our Maker has deliberately permitted His children to feel innate insecurity that we might insistently and instinctively feel
an inner tug toward Him as surely as the salmon
feels that mysterious pull toward the place of his
origin.

To overcome this insecurity we have created
false gods. And they are sophisticated, to match
our sophisticated time!

The *Self* is, supremely, the god offered to us by
today's unbelieving generation. The religion of this
god is "secularism." It seeks to offer the self as the
god who can pacify the turbulent subconscious insecurities. This modern paganism produces an arrogant self-confidence which ultimately fails. The follower is told to affirm to himself: "I can do all
things myself, for I am strong and mighty and
powerful!" The follower of this unchristian faith
berates a supernatural religion as something only
for weaklings. "Only weak men need an outside
God," the civilized pagan proudly boasts.

In the "religion" of secularism, self-indulgence
becomes the supreme sacrament. Through clever
manipulations of mental mechanisms of adjust-
ment the educated heathen manages to convince
himself that he is living a "good life." He is
frankly amused at those evangelists who talk about
salvation, sin, and a Saviour. The suggestion of an
eternal judgment does not disturb him. After all,
he is "living a good life." All the while the words of

William E. Henley keep repeating themselves through his self-centered mind:

> *It matters not how straight the gate,*
> *How charged with punishments the scroll;*
> *I am the master of my fate,*
> *I am the captain of my soul.*

In this religion, too, prayers are answered. The man who worships the god of self frequently gets what he wants. The tragedy, however, is that what he gets does not satisfy the deeper longings of his soul. And instead of creating self-esteem, his self-indulgence only leads to a loss of self-respect. Pride gives way to shame. Success is followed by remorse and a hollow feeling of futility and cynicism.

The *State* is another popular god being offered to the twentieth century's insecure man. This modern religion might be called Statism. It bombards us with the propaganda that the state must play the role of God, feeding the hungry, caring for the ill, providing for every need from the cradle to the grave. In short, statism promises complete security from social dangers. It promises a great new age where the human ills that have blighted man will be eliminated by the state.

But every god always demands a price for providential care. And the price is always loss of human freedom. The inherent peril in the modern cult of statism is the surrender of individual freedom to a god who will be kind and beneficent only as long as the men in positions of power are "good" men. In this popular paganism, man is ultimately asked to surrender true freedom in exchange for false security. A catastrophic agreement! Too late he discovers that *security without freedom is man's greatest insecurity!*

Statism suggests that government must solve the national and international problems. Meanwhile there is an increasing tendency to look to "our father" in Washington or to the United Nations to "give us this day our daily bread." Frightened and insecure people are subconsciously singing:

> *Be not dismayed whate'er betide,*
> *The State will take care of you....*
> *Through every day, o'er all the way,*
> *It will take care of you.*

The Christian, however, does not find his security by losing his freedom. Rather, by finding his freedom in Christ he gains security. He surrenders claim to ownership of his private property to God and considers himself only a steward or manager of the goods, gifts and gold that God has permitted to come into his hands. He achieves inner security because he can trust God completely and always, for he believes that God is sinless and holy and just and merciful and that all things work together for the good of those who love Him.

The *Scientist* is the god of still another segment of society. The image of the man in the white coat in the spotless lab is that of one who is omnipotent and omniscient. Pronouncements that are made by prominent scientists are viewed as authoritative. "Scientism" becomes the new religion of an unbelieving generation. This is most conspicuous in those nations controlled by a dialectical materialistic philosophy. The scientist is a god in Russia.

Even in America we are tempted to be overly impressed by the accomplishments of science.

To illustrate the problem: Science speaks and we believe! A medical doctor by the name of Joseph Salk declares that a vaccine has been produced which effects immunity from polio. It is admittedly not 100 percent effective. In fact, there have been cases where the vaccine was administered and still the disease was contracted. But in an overwhelming number of cases those patients who were vaccinated have developed an immunity. So says science. And we believe it. I believe it. So do you! We are convinced that the vaccine has been proven effective.

Now, by the very same reasoning I declare that there is a supernatural God who hears and answers prayer. No less a person then Jesus Christ announced that if people would pray in the right manner, God in heaven would answer their prayers. The same skeptic who believes Dr. Salk quietly disbelieves the claim of Christ. Why? Because prayer has not been tried? On the contrary—prayer has been tried for 2000 years and the accumulated testimonies are far more impressive than the records Dr. Salk can marshall in defense of his polio vaccine! The skeptic answers, "Well, of course, there have been amazing incidents; but they would have occurred anyway. There is no proof that prayer made the difference." But by the same reasoning there is no *proof* that all who developed an immunity to polio following the innoculation developed this immunity because of the vaccine! Our problem is that we are strongly inclined to accept as verified knowledge any pronouncement made by a scientist with the proper degrees from an accredited university. But we hesitate to show the same respect for and trust in the teachings of our Lord!

We are in great danger of making the scientist the sacred cow of a skeptical society.

Santayana, American philosopher and poet, wrote:

> *O world, thou choosest not the better part!*
> *It is not wisdom to be only wise,*
> *And on the inward vision close the eyes;*
> *But it is wisdom to believe the heart.*
> *Columbus found a world, and had no chart*
> *Save one that faith deciphered in the skies;*
> *To trust the soul's invincible surmise*
> *Was all his science and his only art.*
> *Our knowledge is a torch of smoky pine*
> *That lights the pathway but one step ahead*
> *Across a void of mystery and dread.*
> *Bid, then, the tender light of faith to shine*
> *By which alone the mortal heart is led*
> *Unto the thinking of the thought divine.*

The truth is that man's insecurities will never be fully removed by the test-tube technician.

Now the first commandment points us to the road to the good life by reminding us that we can overcome our insecurity if we will follow the *Saviour's* God—the God who gave these Ten Commandments, the invisible One who flung burning stars, searing suns, and spinning satellites soaring through space: who in the misty dawn of creation breathed into a glorified mass of dust the human spirit. This all powerful, all-knowing, all-wise, everywhere-present God is the God that Jesus worshiped!

Now the Christian religion is completely confident that the God whom Jesus trusted is the True God who alone is able to still the inner tremblings and turmoils of insecurity. As Augustine said, "Our souls are restless, O Lord, until they rest in Thee."

If the first commandment says anything to us today it is this: O quivering, frightened world, behold and believe in the God of the Christ! The Saviour's God is the only source of inner security!

Get acquainted with the God and Father of our Lord Jesus Christ. Discover how He hears and answers prayer. Find out how He listens, and loves, and lifts. Discover how quietly He guides, guards, and undergirds! Then, like all the truly free men of the past centuries, you will find the Lord to be your God. Then you will exclaim with David, "The Lord is my shepherd; I shall not want."

Somehow we must learn that what we need most of all today are not more *new things*. We have enough gadgets now to enslave us. We find ourselves losing our freedom to the tyranny of things: The house says, "Repair me." The car shouts, "Wash me." The clothes cry out and demand, "Press me." We are already slaves to things.

Nor do we need new ideas. Some would-be solver of national and international problems thinks that what we need are some fresh imaginative ideas to solve man's problems. Secretly it is hoped that a brilliant new creative idea will pop up in some super-intellectual brain that will guide the world to everlasting peace.

The truth is that the big wonderful idea has already been thought of. What we need is not the discovery of new *things* or new *ideas*, but a rediscovery of the grand and glorious revelation to a sad

and sick humanity 2000 years ago. My insecure
friend, follow Christ, who came to lead humanity
to the only true God.

God has spoken. He has drawn the curtain. He
has opened the door. He has allowed us to catch a
glimpse of Himself in the quiet tall Stranger of
Galilee who hangs limp on a Roman cross. He, the
wounded God, is the personification of the big idea
that can save our world and give men the inner security they crave.

The Second Commandment:
"Thou shalt not make unto thee any
graven image"

How can I know what God is like? What image can I intelligibly believe to be an authentic impression, a responsible representation, a reliable image? Here, honest seeker, is the Perfect Portrait! Here is the image of integrity. For the Christian Gospel is the good news that God gave the world a perfect portrait and an immaculate image of Himself. God came down and walked around on this earth in a human body. And He was called Jesus! This Christ is not an ordinary itinerant preacher. This is God putting Himself in our shoes. It was the only way God could "get through" to the human race.

Chapter Two

FIND OUT WHAT GOD
IS REALLY LIKE

He was a distinguished and apparently successful man. He stepped into our church office with that "Where is God, please" look on his face. He candidly announced that he wanted God! He spoke with the matter-of-fact manner of a man in a drugstore asking for a bottle of aspirin.

He had, at least, and at last, discovered that the good life is something you can't buy. He knew that inner security, peace in depth, is something that can be found only in a vital encounter with the living God. He was out to discover and find God for himself—life's supreme adventure.

Now, there are two pitfalls that must be carefully avoided by the man who is going out to "get religion" and "find God."

First, there is the danger of finding the wrong god. There are a variety of religions in the world today. Certainly not all can be right. So the first commandment is the call to choose the right God— the God that Jesus Christ worshiped.

The second danger in "finding God" is the peril of misunderstanding Him. It is no wonder there are agnostics in the world. The immature image of God presented by some religious teachers is understandably offensive to intelligent minds.

It is precisely at this point that the second commandment becomes relevant. "Thou shalt not make ... any graven images" is not only a stern commandment, but good advice as well.

Now there is little danger that any reader of this book will carve idols and pray to man-made gods of wood or ivory or stone. Some months ago I stood in the heart of Baalbek, that ancient city just west of Damascus, in the Middle East. In the ruins of the pagan temple you can see and touch the stones that were worshiped by primitive people. Certainly we are too sophisticated today to do as they did. Yes, but we are in greater danger of violating this command by carving, creating, and coddling in our mind false images of God, which distort, destroy, and desecrate the authentic image of the Eternal One.

What is the image of God you have graven in your mind?

Let us look at some of the graven images sculptured by the imaginations of men.

I

The *Grand Patriarch* is one of the more prevalent perverted images of God. This false image visualizes God as a Grand Old Man with a silver beard, in some respects not unlike Santa Claus in appearance, except that He is more stately and dignified, and definitely more serious. But in character we imagine Him very much like the legendary benefactor who comes around at Christmas and promiscuously bestows His gifts upon good little boys and girls.

No wonder that some people cannot honestly believe in God! The maturing mind discovers that there is no Santa Claus after all—it is only a beautiful make-believe story, a lovely legend, tender fiction—and not a few thinking men have, mistakenly, suspected the teaching concerning God they received in childhood as they begin to discard the false belief in Santa Claus.

The thinking Christian avoids this pitfall. He does not visualize God as a gentle Grandfather who spoils his grandchildren by giving them anything they want. Life has a way of sternly upsetting such an impression of God. For we see "good people" suffer, apparently legitimate prayers go unanswered, and problems in the lives of Christian people remaining like thorns in the flesh. No, the image of God as a Grand Old Patriarch who lavishly spends his time keeping his children and grandchildren and great-grandchildren happy and laughing is a gross distortion. God is not a soft-hearted old man too tender to administer discipline or to punish the arrogant and rebellious child.

I recall one intelligent young man who told me that as a child he believed in Santa Claus and God but that he had discovered that *both* are make-believe. His was a false and fatal leap in logic! Of course, we do not believe in Santa Claus, for there is no evidence of his existence. But if there were packages left in homes around the world every year at Christmas, and all of the best investigators and scientists and astronomers were unable to explain where these gifts came from; and if there were an unbroken traditional testimony that way back in history people of unquestionable integrity in large numbers had seen a man with a white beard soaring through the skies dropping these gifts at Christmas—then, of course, we might believe in Santa Claus.

We believe in God because we see evidences of His invisible power and might and glory in the world and in the lives of people. No one can explain for certain where the world came from or how it got here although there are a variety of "theories." We are reasonably sure that once there was nothing—now there is something.

There is, in fact, a whole universe.

As a building presupposes an architect, and a painting presupposes an artist, and a poem presupposes a poet, so the universe presupposes a Grand Architect of the ages. If I saw footprints on the beach, I would conclude that someone had been there. God's footprints are clearly seen on the shores of the immeasurable universe.

If I walked into the desert and saw a pile of rocks, I would think nothing of it. If I walked in the desert and saw a long ridge of rocks, I would think nothing of it. If I walked in the desert and saw a rock here and another there, I would think nothing of it. But if, in the middle of the desert, I came upon a neat arrangement of rocks lying in rows with one rock in the first row, two in the second row, three in the third row, four in the fourth row, five in the fifth row, and six rocks in the sixth row, and all of the rows arranged one above the other to form a perfect triangle—I would intelligently conclude that someone had been there. That is the way our universe has been put together.

Yes, there is so much evidence for a Master Mind in the universe that we can say that the reality and the existence of God is proven by the normal scientific methods of reasoning.

But let us make sure that our image of this living God is true and valid.

II

God is also often imagined as the *Grim Patrolman*. A certain girl had this impression. When asked what God was like, she answered, "Someone who is always watching to see if I am doing anything wrong." In such minds God is pictured as the Grim Patrolman of the universe, armed with a gruesome assortment of weapons and means to keep the world humble and submissive. Lightning, famine, earthquakes, sliding ice floes—all are attributed to the "wrath of God."

But the very God-spirit within us rejects this revolting concept of the Almighty. We make a serious mistake, it seems to me, if we identify God with nature. He is free and above the laws of nature. Certainly God is not mean, vindictive, and brutal! John Calvin, that great churchman, said: "Faith is an asssurance of the goodness of God."

III

There are others who view God as the *Great Politician*. He is imagained as one who manipulates nations, watches for His opportunity and then mercilessly "uses people" only to drop them mercilessly when He has what He wants.

God is no politician, no cheap opportunist. Some people confuse providence with politics, but God is certainly not responsible for the sins of the human race and the resulting wars and tragedies.

But what is true is that in His glorious providence He redeems miserable situations so that tragedies become triumphs, burdens become blessings, obstacles become opportunities, and problems become possibilities. Just take a look at the cross of Christ on Easter morning!

IV

So you rightly and wisely ask, How can I know what God is like? What image can I intelligently believe to be an authentic impression, a responsible representation, a reliable image?

Here, honest seeker, is the *Glorious Portrait*! Here is the image of integrity. For the Christian Gospel is the good news that God gave the world a perfect portrait and an immaculate image of Himself. Behold the Babe of Bethlehem.

God came down and walked around on this earth in a human body. And He was called Jesus! This Christ is not an ordinary itinerant preacher. This is

God putting Himself in our shoes. It was the only way God could "get through" to the human race.

Father Damien, you remember, was a great missionary to the lepers. From the first he called them his brothers and sisters. But he did not establish a real rapport with them until years later, when he addressed them with the words, "We lepers"! Christ was God, getting down to our level. The Babe in the manger is God wrapped in a blanket—royalty in rags. The stranger of Galilee performing those unexplainable miracles (which even His enemies never doubted or disqualified)—this tall man with the compassionate heart—is God with a robe on, God with sandals on His feet, God eating bread and drinking water and becoming tired. This is God, putting Himself into our shoes in order to portray clearly to the human family what He, the Eternal, is really like!

Once, Philip asked Jesus, "Lord, shew us the Father," and Jesus replied, "Have I been so long time with you, and yet hast thou not known me, Philip? he that hath seen me hath seen the Father" (John 14:9).

Yes, draw close to Christ and you will have the perfect portrait, the only divinely approved image of the Almighty God.

And what kind of God do you see when you look at His image in Christ? You see first a God who guides. As a lad, I had a little boat which I pulled with a string around in circles in a large tank of water. God does not pull us like a boy pulls a boat tied on a string. I also recall the early spring days in Iowa when we would walk a mile home to our farm from the country school. The ditches along the country roads had been filled with drifting snow in the winter. The warm spring sun would melt the snow and create little streams in the ditches. We boys used to put a little four-inch twig in the stream at the schoolhouse and guide the little "boat" all the way home. Sometimes it would become snagged and with a long stick we would gently prod it loose and send it freely on its way again. God guides you with enthusiasm and intense interest when you give your life over to Him.

And all the while, He provides. "The Lord is my Shepherd, I shall not want," was David's faith. This is the grand image of God that we see in the perfect portrait of Him in Jesus Christ. For our Lord promised, "Ask, and ye shall receive. . . ." And again to assure us that God would not only guide but provide, Jesus said, "Behold the fowls of the air: they sow not, neither do they reap, nor gather into barns; yet your heavenly Father feedeth them. Are ye not much better than they? . . . And why take ye thought for raiment? Consider the lilies of the field, how they grow; they toil not, neither do they spin. And yet I say unto you, That even Solomon in all his glory was not arrayed like one of these. Wherefore, if God so clothe the grass of the field . . . shall he not much more clothe you, O ye of little faith? . . . your heavenly Father knoweth that ye have need of all these things" (Matt. 6:26-32).

There you have it! God knows what you need and your legitimate needs will be provided. That is the kind of God Christ presented to the world.

Of course, *we* get our needs and our wants all mixed up. We consider to be necessities what are, in reality, luxuries. There are only four absolutely basic human needs. We need water, food, and air, or our body will die. Without these things we cannot live. And we need forgiveness of our sins, and all that comes with it, otherwise our soul shall never enjoy spiritual life. These needs God will supply.

But there is no promise that He will give us what we want. Not infrequently, we do not know what we want. For example, we think we want a new car. In reality we want an escape from boredom, and the car "kick" constitutes a new interest, a new "cause," a new absorbing project. I venture an analysis that more often than not we really do not want the "thing" we are buying. What we really want is the joy of shopping, the venture of running around to break the cabin fever; or we buy to make an impression. And, too often, what we want is not the best for us. No wonder God in His mercy neglects so often to provide what we want.

Christ portrays a God who guides us through life, provides us with what we need, and *abides with us forever*. There is no promise that God will never allow His children to experience pain, or suffering, or even fall victim to natural catastrophies. But there is the promise that He will be with us always and everywhere. The Psalmist knew this. And he said, "Yea, though I walk through the valley of the shadow of death, I will fear no evil: *for thou art with me*."

Hear the Word of the Lord: "Fear not; for I have redeemed you, I have called you by your name and you are mine! When you pass through the waters . . . they shall not overflow you . . . fear not, for I am with you" (Isa. 43:1, 2, 5).

Once Livingstone was asked how he was able to face the steaming jungles, months of loneliness, dangers of beast, serpent, insect, disease, and savages. The great missionary testified to the University of Glasgow where he was receiving an honorary degree of Doctor of Laws, "Would you like me to tell you what supported me through all the years of exile among people whose language I could not understand, and whose attitude toward me was always uncertain and often hostile? It was this—" He paused reverently. His left arm, crushed by a lion's jaws, hung limp and helpless at his side. Then he continued,—"It was this, 'Lo, I am with you alway, even unto the end of the world.' On these words I staked everything, and they never failed!"

Come close, friend.

Draw near, neighbor.

Follow me, wayfarer. Take a serious, sincere, and searching look at Christ, and you will have an authentic image of the Eternal God. And while you look, bend your knee and kneel. . . .

The Third Commandment:
"Thou shalt not take the name
of the Lord thy God in vain"

What is God's appeal here? It is this: "I am the Lord thy God"—listen to Me, take My Word seriously. I cannot give you peace, or poise, or power, if you will not take My word, My will, My way seriously and sincerely. It is precisely at this point that this ancient commandment becomes impressively up-to-date. Our generation is infected with a variety of anxiety illnesses. If a patient neglects to take the full dose of medicine prescribed by his doctor, the latter is no longer responsible for the patient's condition. And if we neglect to take God's Word seriously, God cannot and will not hold us guiltless. He will hold us responsible for our own predicament.

Chapter Three

THEN TAKE
GOD SERIOUSLY

One of the most amazing moments in time—and I might add, one of the most terrifying moments in history, occurred 964 years ago.

For a close look at the scene, we roll the calendar back to the year 999. Christianity was now nearly one thousand years old. The promise of our Lord that He would return again to the earth was understood to be fulfilled after a thousand years. And for centuries, Christians believed that if Christ did not return before the millennium, cer-

tainly He would return to this earth at the crack of
the dawn of the new millennium. Suspense mount-
ed as the years rolled on—990, 991, 992, 993,
994, 995, 996, 997, 998, 999—and with the birth
of what by many was supposed to be the last year
of life on this planet, strange and amazing things
began to happen. People began to listen to their
church with a wholehearted seriousness. There was
no stealing. Cheating was almost unknown. Bakers
gave bread away free. There was a constant cycle
of confessions, absolutions, masses and commu-
nions.

An ancient chronicle describes what supposedly
took place on the last day. As midnight neared,
masters and servants embraced. Offenders forgave
each other. There was open repentance and godly
sorrow for sin. In the old basilica of St. Peter,
Pope Sylvester II performed a midnight mass in
silence. The church was jammed. Inside, a huge
clock ticked once each second. The Pope prayed in
silence. The worshipers lay face down, afraid to
look up. Suddenly, the clock stopped ticking. Hun-
dreds shrieked. Some died of fright. The bell began
to strike the midnight hour. Pope Sylvester raised
his hands. All the bells rang at once. From the
choir loft came *Te Deum Laudamus*—To God Be
Glory!

Now, they obviously erred in their interpretation
of the promises of Christ concerning His return to
this earth. But they did not err in the keeping of
the third commandment. For at least they were not
taking the name of God in vain. Certainly, they
were taking God seriously for a moment.

And they have left an invaluable illustration of
what can happen in the world if men will, with so-

ber and sincere hearts, take the name of God seriously. This is the positive application of this commandment.

You are familiar with its negative implication: Cursing, swearing, coarse talk, shoddy conversation, smelly language, gutter vocabulary are forbidden for God's people. Profanity is the language of skid row, prison cells, cheap bars and harlots' lairs. Let us not belabor the painful point that profanity is pitifully prevalent today. You already know this. And you know, too, that profanity is a sin.

When a famous and respectable citizen decides to "give 'em hell," he does not dignify profanity but rather he desecrates his own person and position.

Every reader of this book has enough intelligence to express himself with intensity without crude cursing. It is still true that profanity is the uncouth effort of a feeble mind to express itself forcibly. Remember, friend, who and what you are! When someone tried to teach a young French prince to use profanity, he stoutly refused with the proud declaration: "I will not say it! I will not say it! I was born to be king, and I will not say it!" To the Christian, let it be said: "You were born to be a saint. You are a child of God. May your language be appropriate to your divine calling!"

But our anxious generation desperately needs to hear the deeper truth. Hear the Word of the Lord: "Thou shalt not take the name of the Lord thy God in vain, for the Lord will not hold him guiltless that taketh his name in vain." What is God's appeal here? It is this: "I am the Lord thy God"— *listen to Me, take My work seriously.* I cannot give you peace, or poise, or power, if you will not take

My word, My will, My way seriously and sincerely.

It is precisely at this point that this ancient commandment becomes impressively up-to-date. Our generation is infected with a variety of anxiety illnesses. If a patient neglects to take the full dose of medicine prescribed by his doctor, the latter is no longer responsible for the patient's condition. And if we neglect to take God's Word seriously, God cannot and will not hold us guiltless. He will hold us responsible for our own predicament.

In the first place, it is high time we learned to take God's warnings seriously. Thou shalt not take the warnings of God in vain. This advice is imperative to anyone who wants to live the good life.

Near Forest Home, high in the California mountains, are beautiful falls. At the foot of these falls is a sign, posted there by the rangers. It says, simply, that the trail ahead is dangerous. It warns that the way to the top is precarious and has often been fatal. "Don't be next!" is the solemn slogan that summarizes the warning. Still, there are the adventurous who will climb to the top of the falls. There is no law against it. You are free to explore. You may challenge the trail. But if you are injured on the way, the rangers and the State of California are not responsible!

Now, here is a timely application. God is not responsible for the plight of the world, or the fright in your life, if His Word has not been seriously heeded. Now it is natural that we do not want to hear and heed the divine warnings. Warnings, by their very nature, are not very inspiring. Warnings are not happy sounds. No wonder we like to ignore them. But listen to His sober warning: "The wages of sin is death." Listen to His sober warning—the sign at the foot of the falls—"The soul that sinneth, it shall die." Listen to His sober warning—the sign at the foot of the falls—"How shall you escape if you neglect God's great salvation?" Listen to the sober warning from the lips of Christ: "He that hears these words of mine and does them not, I will liken him unto a foolish man who built his house on sand, and the rains descended and the floods came and the winds blew and beat upon that house and it fell, and great was the fall of it!"

So sounds the ominous statement of the Saviour Himself. Of course, these are not pleasant words. But for the sake of our immortal soul we had better take God's warnings seriously—or suffer the consequences. The height of self-deceit is when a person tells himself that he can sin and that God will automatically forgive and forget—that somehow, "nature" will overlook the whole affair. The terrible truth is that judgment is built into the universe.

God has posted signs at the foot of the falls. They are given not to frighten but to guide; not to instill fear, but to prevent catastrophe. Look, listen, and live!

Furthermore, we take God's promises in vain. No wonder our trembling world is so frightened! Let's have an honest understanding. God is not the inventor of fear. He is not responsible for our worry, fear, and anxiety. It's our own fault. If we took God's promises seriously, we would mount up with wings like eagles, run and not be weary, walk and never faint.

For instance, take the man who can't get to sleep at night and tosses in his bed. First, he begins to worry that he might not fall asleep. And then he

thinks that if he doesn't get to sleep, he's not going
to have the strength to do his job. He is going to
crack up, he fearfully imagines, and his career will
be ruined. So his imagination works overtime and
before he knows it, he has fabricated a terrifying ghost that haunts his mind, and robs him of the
joy of living! What he needs is spiritual therapy.
Let him read some of God's wonderful promises of
peace and love and power and in quietness of mind
he will rest in a natural sleep. Quietly, gently, ten-
derly, let the promise of God fall softly and
sweetly into your tense, tight mind: "Thou wilt
keep him in perfect peace whose mind is stayed on
thee." "Peace I give unto you—let not your heart
be troubled, neither let it be afraid." "I am the Lord
your God." Reach for your Bible, friend, and un-
derline the positive promises of God and trust
them. Indescribable peace is bound to follow!

Last week I held the hand of a very sick woman
who was in her seventies. I was there on Friday
and I was there again on Saturday. She lies criti-
cally ill on a hospital bed. I prayed with her. I
looked deep into her eyes and saw the soul of this
saint. And I saw faith, and confidence, and no fear
at all. No fear at all! She's taking God's promises
seriously; she believes what she reads in her Bible.

The problem with today's Christian is that he is
taking God's promises in vain. God has promised
not only to forgive every sin, but also to guide and
keep us from the cradle until we enter into the
glory of eternity. I recall a Christian friend of mine
who took his religion seriously. On his deathbed,
following a lengthy bout with cancer, he held the
hand of his mother in one of his and the hand of
his wife in the other. Moments before his soul

slipped into that other, dazzling world, he dropped the hands of his mother and his wife, folded his hands upon his chest, and, with an expression of indescribable peace, moved triumphantly on. If you don't take God's promises seriously, He is not responsible for your fears and your worries and your mental distress.

I can understand why men take God's warnings and God's promises in vain. But why do we take God's *invitations* in vain? If you received in the mail an engraved invitation from the President of the United States to be a guest at his table in the White House, you would take it seriously, I am sure. And that is an understatement! We have an invitation to sit at God's table, to receive salvation from our sins through Jesus Christ. This is the great invitation: "Come unto me, all you who labor and are heavy laden, and I will give you rest."

Listen to Him! How winsome! How warm! How welcoming! How wonderful!

This is God, inviting you—now! This is God, inviting you—who suffer with inner shame, and regret and remorse; with hands that are not clean, hearts that are not pure, a mind that has been defiled, and a soul that is sick. This is for you! God is saying: "Come let us reason together. Though your sins be as scarlet, they shall be as white as snow. Though they be red like crimson, they shall be as wool."

The very name of Jesus is an invitation to life abundant and eternal. And we take this name and this gospel in vain. The Bible says that Jesus Christ is not dead—that He still lives. And I believe it. Jesus Christ is alive. He confronts the world and invites mankind to come and accept Him as Saviour and Lord, but we smile politely and don't take

Him too seriously. Mind you, when you do, your immortal soul is redeemed. Your destiny is secure. The Eternal becomes your God and God *your* Father!

One of the great men I have had the privilege of knowing in my life is Dr. Irwin J. Lubbers, former president of Hope College in Holland, Michigan. Dr. Lubbers related recently *the* great experience of his life. He no longer has any real problems with fear, worry and anxiety. Of course, there are the normal tensions that go along with getting your job done. But the deeper, disturbing anxieties, the haunting fears are gone—gone completely. He lives a victorious life and it all happened one day in the winter time. He and his little son, Arend, then twelve years old, were traveling from Michigan, to Central College in Pella, Iowa. On their return trip, the beautiful, clean, clear, hard-surfaced road suddenly changed to ice. Without warning, and before he knew what happened, Dr. Lubbers completely lost control of his car. It overturned and landed in the ditch. He was unconscious, he knows not how long, lying in the cold snow and sleet. Suddenly, revived by the snow and the bitter freezing air, he regained consciousness and saw his little son holding him up. The lad had his little arm under his father's armpits and was lifting his daddy's heavy chest to his own little chest. And in a boyish prayer, his tears falling on the cold face of his gravely injured father, he sobbed, "Dear Jesus, don't let my daddy die. He has lived a good life, and he's tried so hard to do what's right. And he's such a good man. Dear Jesus, don't let my daddy die." "Then," Dr. Lubbers said, "I saw The Presence! There He was, right next to Arend, my son. And there was no

form or comeliness that we should desire Him.
There He was! And I looked at Him and He
looked at me and I wanted to go with Him. The at-
traction was so strong; the tug was so powerful!"

Jesus Christ is alive. Millions have felt His
touch. Thousands of reliable believers have seen
Him. I have had authentic experiences with Him. I
know He is truly alive!

Quietly, Jesus Christ comes to you. Rarely, indeed, does He give to one of His children the privilege of catching a vision of Him. But often He
comes to our mind in a warm and wonderful way
and urges us to take fresh stock of our life and allow Him to convert us and save us forevermore.

For when you take God's Word seriously, you
are well on the road to the Good Life.

The Fourth Commandment:
"Remember the sabbath day, to keep it holy"

A careful study would show that the increase of tension and anxiety illnesses in America is related to the widespread neglect by Americans to set aside one day each week for silence and worship. "In quietness and confidence shall be thy strength" God's Word says. In the brilliance of divine planning, the Creator scheduled one day in seven as a time for the tense, tired, troubled man to strengthen his soul in worship.

Chapter Four

AND KEEP IN CONSTANT TOUCH WITH HIM

If you have trouble with inner tension then this chapter is for you!

You can learn to relax under pressure. You can triumph over inner tension. You can have peace of mind—provided you live God's way.

Here is God's prescription for people under pressure: "Take one day in seven—set it aside to rest the mind, to fill the soul with faith, and to recreate the energy of the body with physical rest."

A careful study would show that the increase of

tension and anxiety illnesses in America is related
to the widespread neglect by Americans to set aside
one day each week for silence and worship.

"In quietness and confidence shall be thy
strength" (Isa. 30:15), God's Word says. In the
brilliance of divine planning, the Creator scheduled
one day in seven as a time for the tense, tired,
troubled man to strengthen his soul in worship.

No commandment, then, is more relevant than
the fourth: "Remember the sabbath day, to keep it
holy. Six days shalt thou labour, and do all thy
work: but the seventh day is the sabbath of the
Lord thy God: in it thou shalt not do any work."

Before we go further, let it be said that this is
one commandment that cannot be taken literally.
In the first place, we are in trouble with the early
church if we attempt to take this fourth commandment literally. For in the book of Acts the early
Christians under the guidance of the Holy Spirit
poured out upon them at Pentecost were divinely
guided to shift the day of worship and rest from
the seventh day to the first day of each week. The
purpose was clear—that Christians might worship
on the day our Lord was resurrected from the
grave. In the glory of the New Testament faith,
baptism replaced circumcision; the Holy Commu-
nion replaced the Passover Feast; and the day of
worship was changed from the seventh day to the
first day—for Christ lives! The Sabbath day became
the Lord's Day.

Furthermore, we are in trouble with some pretty
hard facts of science if we attempt to interpret this
command in an extreme literal manner. God, apparently, did not make the world in six twenty-
four-hour periods. I respect the opinion of those

who suppose that this is the meaning of the word "day" in Genesis, but the same Scriptures remind us that "a day in the sight of God is as a thousand years." Indeed, the preponderance of scholarship seems to support the view that God made the world as He does everything else—majestically slow, magnificently silent, divinely patient, He unfolded His creative plan.

Obviously, a literal interpretation of this command will get us into trouble with our times, although I must admit that we are in trouble with our times, no matter how we seek to apply this rule for living. It is quite obvious that it is impossible in a sinful world for all work to stop. Doctors, policemen, and a variety of public servants are naturally called upon to do their labor on every day of the week.

Finally, we are in trouble with ourselves if we follow the letter instead of the spirit of this commandment. The rule would then become a burden instead of a blessing. Instead of a day of rest, it would become a day of tension and strain. Fortunately, we have a generous and wise word from our Lord who was Himself rebuked by religious extremists: "the sabbath was made for man," He said, "not man for the sabbath" (Mark 2:27).

The Sabbath was made for you. Yes, that means that Sunday is God's gift for tired, tense, tempted, troubled souls. Therefore, we do not fill it with negative restrictions, though there is no doubt that if Jesus Christ should visit this earth today, He would have a few negative things to say.

America's misuse and abuse of this God-given gift of one day in seven for worship and rest is well known. A holy day has become a holiday. Sunday has become Funday. Indeed, America has wandered far afield from the early founding days when Sunday was a quiet day, when the stores were closed and places of public entertainment were not open. It was a day for the Church and it was a day for the family. It was a day of rest and peace. Now, I submit that there is a causal relationship between America's desecration of the Sabbath and the widespread anxiety illnesses that are sweeping our country. I am thoroughly convinced that an overwhelming number of mental and emotional illnesses stem directly or indirectly from the failure of the American people to observe God's gift of Sunday in a positive and creative manner. At this point, I give a testimony: I attribute to a great degree the mental and the emotional and spiritual health that I enjoy to my childhood training in Sunday observance. I have only beautiful, happy childhood memories of Sunday. And every Sunday morning when the sun comes up, even to this day, I subconsciously relive for a moment in my memory those happy childhood Sunday mornings. And in this reliving, my mind feels good. And what were Sundays like for me? First of all, Sunday was a day of quietness. Offensive, strident, irritating noises were not allowed around our farm house. The roar of tractors and the blast of popular music were frankly forbidden. Every Sunday morning we heard organ music from the radio, birds singing in the trees, and church bells tolling in the distance. And when we did something, as a family, it was never in a situation where our minds and nerves were grated by the grinding sounds of contemporary life. We did not discuss controversial matters in our family on Sunday. Situations that had within them the potential to create strain and stress and tension were deliberately and carefully avoided. My father would say: "It can wait until tomorrow . . . it can wait. . . ." Sunday was a day of peace and quietness.

When passing Sunday-evening traffic, I often study the faces of the people in their cars. Sometimes I see a family that's laughing together. Mother is turning to the back seat, joking and smiling with the children. They seem to be having a wonderful time. You can see they have been to church. It has been so good for them. But there are others; their hair is disheveled; their haggard faces are tense and the nervous driver grips the wheel tightly in the bumper-to-bumper traffic. His wife, sitting in front, turns around with strained face to shout at quarreling children. They have spent their Sunday foolishly. Now, they are hot, tired, irritable. Plan your Sunday in such a way that it will be a day of rest and quietness.

And then, for us at least, Sunday was a day which was absolutely different—and I'm grateful for it, even though I used to grumble and complain that I couldn't go fishing on Sundays. There was a river that ran through the back of our Iowa farm and it seemed that so often Sunday morning was a specially quiet morning. The air hardly moved and I knew that over the deep holes in the back of the river the water was quiet, tranquil, and calm, and if I could just drop a hook and line in there, I'd be able to see the slightest nibble. And, oh, how I wanted to fish on Sundays! But, it was forbidden for me. I looked across the street and watched the neighborhood boys with their fishing poles over their shoulders and the can of worms in their left

hands, walking off to the river to catch the big
ones. But I had to go to Sunday school every Sunday. And I had to go to church. Just as I had to
brush my teeth and go to public school. And at the
time I complained—I know I did; but today I have
only happy childhood memories. I thank God for
it. It was a day of quietness and a day of peace.
And it was a day of fun. But the fun was centered
in the church and in the family. We never spent
money to have fun on Sundays. Of course, we took
our offerings to church and Sunday school, but they
were not payments. And we discovered, as many of
you have, I know, that you have the most fun
when you don't spend any money at all. It's still
true that the best things in life are free.

Perhaps the communities in America will begin
to sense that the commercializing of Sunday has
spoiled the spirit of the day and we long for the
time that we shall see the community spirit react
and redemptively revolt, saying: "This is enough!
Let's keep this day for the family and the church."
All sorts of social forces are at work to disrupt the
natural bond between fathers, mothers, and children.

There is something almost spiritual about driving through some of these quiet little towns in
America today, where the people are dressed for
church. Let it be a day for worship.

And let it be a day for the family. If any
member of the family, father, mother, or child,
has a hobby which would disrupt or disect the
family circle, this hobby should be reconsidered
seriously. Draw plans for Sunday which will draw
the family closer together. This is why God gave
the day to you. Sunday is God's gift. Invest it—

don't spend it! Husbands and wives, take time to talk. Fathers, have dialogue with your children; listen to them; find out what they've been doing during the past week. Get out of your world of worries and projects and ambitions and drives and get into the world of your little children. I have a friend who likes to play golf. He tells this story: "One day I was going out. Just as I was putting the golf clubs in the car, I looked at the front door of my house and there was my little tiny, curly-haired boy, his big eyes filling with tears as he pleaded: 'Can't I go with you, Daddy? Please?' I said, 'No, you can't go with me on the golf course.' He shed some more tears and I drove off, leaving him standing sad and lonely at the screen door. I went on to play golf. But the face of my little boy haunted me. I decided then and there to wait a few years with my golf. I turned around and drove home. I will never forget the happy sound of my son, shouting with delight as I pulled into the driveway. 'Daddy's home! Mommy, Daddy came home for me!' Today I take my children to church and Sunday school and our family life is wonderful!"

Sunday is a gift of God. Find it; discover it; live by it. And remember, Sunday is a 24-hour day. Sunday doesn't start at 9:30 and stop right after Sunday dinner. It does not. I remember walking recently into a beautiful modern hotel in Israel. It was on a Friday morning when we stepped into the luxurious lobby of this modern hotel and saw a sign, right in the middle of the lobby, which read: "The Sabbath begins today at 6:16." That was the time of sundown, of course. And the next day the sign was changed to read: "The Sabbath ends today at 6:16." The Jewish people, at least, have been wisely taught. The Sabbath is a twenty-four-hour period. Now there is a good reason for this. We need a twenty-four-hour rest physically, mentally and spiritually. Any man who tries to get by with less is going to die at too early an age, or will find himself the victim of mental or emotional or spiritual sicknesses. It is a law of God that is built into the universe.

You were made in such a way that you have what it takes to face life's struggle. And you have what it takes to face life's problems. And you have what it takes to face life's worries—provided that every seven days you fill up your soul with faith!

Live this way. You'll find a peace and power you never knew before.

PART II: BUILD YOUR LIFE AROUND YOUR RELIGION

The Fifth Commandment:
"Honor thy father and thy mother"

Parents are symbols of a culture and a heritage. There is a tragic tendency in each generation to disrespect its moral and spiritual inheritance. Such disrespect for heritage and culture can be repeated from one generation to the next until, in a period of less than one hundred years, an entire nation can lose its heritage which was centuries slow in evolving. In one generation a whole way of life can be lost.

Chapter Five

THE GOOD LIFE BEGINS
IN THE HOME

Probably the greatest problem facing most people today lies in the realm of public relations. If we could learn to live in love and peace with our neighbor, we would be well on the road to the good life. It is essential and imperative that we cultivate the skill and acquire the art of getting along with people.

The average person cannot be a hermit in the hills and take the attitude, "I don't care what people think of me." It so happens that we are social creatures. Man is innately gregarious. That means we're not happy unless we are around people.

Consequently it is imperative that we cultivate the art of living in harmony with people around us.

Significantly the Ten Commandments were originally divided into two tablets. The first tablet includes the four commandments which deal with man's relationship to God. The second tablet lists six commandments that deal with man's relationship to his fellow men. You might say that the Ten Commandments, in summary, have two broad lessons to teach us. The first is: If you want to live a good life, get religion. And the second is: Live this religion. Practice what you preach. Learn to get along with people.

To start us off, we have in the fifth commandment, "Honor thy father and thy mother." For the home is the first classroom where we learn the primary lessons in good human relations. If you con't get along with the people in your home, don't be surprised if you have trouble with the people in the office.

Now the fifth commandment should be taken quite literally. It means that the youngster must respect and honor his father and his mother. It means that the teen-ager must respect and honor his father and mother. It means that the newly-married young man must continue to honor and respect his father and his mother. And it means that the middle-aged person whose father and mother now are very old and probably bordering on senility must still honor and respect his father and his mother. It is regrettably true that in not a few instances this commandment is violated more by people in their forties and fifties than by the teenagers. Honor and respect your father and mother until they go to their graves and then continue to honor and respect them with at least an occasional tribute.

Remember the law of proportionate return. "Cast your bread upon the waters and it shall return." "Whatsoever a man sows, that shall he also reap." Jesus put it this way, "With what measure you mete, it will be meted to you again." The way you treat your old father and mother is the way your children will treat you when you are old. Life treats us the way we treat life. This is the law of proportionate return.

But there is a more profound lesson implied in this fifth rule for good living. We are not only to honor and respect father and mother because they are our parents, but we must also respect and honor the timeless virtues that father and mother symbolize.

I

Now the father is first a symbol of law and authority. In the home the child first learns that he is not a free person. His appetites, instincts, drives and urges cannot have free license and reign. There are God-given laws that must be honored. So the father soon becomes the symbol of law. Now the child who does not learn to respect the law is a person who has not learned a fundamental lesson for good living. Furthermore, the father and mother are symbols of authority. Authority is the right to judge and to enforce the law. And this is what a child must learn in the home. He must learn that breaking laws will result in judgment. And judgment will be reflected in retributive punishment. This is a reason why the Bible declares so emphatically, "Spare the rod and spoil the child."

Of course, judgment always follows broken laws. There was the little boy whose mother was a child psychologist, and who had her own concept of authority. It wasn't the Biblical concept at all. It was another kind, the roses-and-lilies-and-perfumed kind of authority, you know. When her son wouldn't eat his breakfast, she said, "Eat your breakfast, Son. Eat your crisp, toasted, brown cereal." He looked at her with a spoiled sneer and said, "Motivate me."

"Honor thy father and thy mother" is a call to honor and respect law and authority.

II

Parents are symbols of a culture and a heritage. There is a tragic tendency in each generation to disrespect its moral and spiritual inheritance. This is first evident in the teen-age years. Suddenly father's ideas, father's philosophy, father's way of living, father's morality is out-dated, old-fashioned and woefully inadequate for "modern living."

Such disrespect for heritage and culture can be repeated from one generation to the next until, in a period of less than one hundred years, an entire nation can lose its heritage which was centuries slow in evolving. In one generation a whole way of life can be lost. Refined tastes, sensitive morals, high principles, great values can be squandered by one careless, crude and undisciplined generation which fails to respect and honor its grand inheritance!

To guard against this, our nation has always

looked for its leadership to men who were educated in the Liberal Arts. No one was considered well educated unless he was trained to appreciate the arts as well as the sciences. Something has happened, however, to America's educational system. Specialization has arrived. And the humanities have largely been forgotten in many universities. So today we find college graduates who do not respect the best of Western culture. The latest popular jazz singer ranks higher than Beethoven. Classical music is sarcastically called "high-brow stuff." And prominent educators dare to challenge our moral, spiritual, economic and cultural heritage. The fifth commandment is a call to America to revive a reverent respect for our glorious Christian heritage!

III

Parents are also symbols of seniority. This commandment does much for us if it reminds us to respect and honor those who have been around longer than we have. Everybody detests the fresh college graduate who steps in and tries to reorganize everything. We all pass through a certain stage of life when we think we know it all and think the gray-haired people are way behind the times. When we have read the latest books and have earned the most advanced degree, then let us pause to remember that there is one quality that can't be learned from books, and that is common sense. This priceless treasure is something that is acquired through years of experience and it has no relationship whatever to the intelligence quotient. Some of the smartest people in the world have demonstrated the most tragic lack of common sense.

Judgment and intelligence don't necessarily go together. Brilliant minds have often demonstrated pitiful judgments on moral, social, spiritual, economic and political issues.

Here is part of our national problem today. Moral leadership has slipped out of the control of a Ten-Commandment-honoring church into the adulterous hands of irresponsible progressives and extreme liberals who through "sophisticated" novels, "realistic" movies, "progressive" classroom lectures, "bold" newspaper columns, and "broadminded" round-table discussions are leading thinking Americans away from the solid shores of immovable moral truth into the murky, muddy swamps and seas of moral liberalism which waits to suck up and swallow any intellectual fool who dares to invent a new moral code.

Read the opinions of some of our intellectuals today on moral issues and it becomes obvious that many brilliant people are moral and spiritual fools. Intelligence and judgment don't always go together. What we desperately need is respect for the wisdom of senior citizens who lived and walked with God.

IV

And, finally, father and mother are the symbols of love. Wise young people know that no human being in the world loves them more than their father and mother. "Honor thy father and thy mother" is another way of saying, "Honor and respect love."

I have met people who seem to think that the compassionate, gentle, tenderhearted man is a sissy or a weakling. Not so! The open heart, not the clenched fist, is the symbol of a good man!

In the home we learn to honor and respect love as the queen of the virtues. "And now abideth faith, hope and love, and the greatest of these is love." So this commandment says, "Don't just respect father and mother as persons, but respect what father and mother symbolize—law, authority, seniority, heritage and love."

Parents, meanwhile, have to *earn* this honor. You can't legislate respect.

I know a father who is doing something he shouldn't be doing. I spoke to him about it. I said, "What's your son going to think?" "Oh," he said, "my children don't know what I do." To which I replied, "Do you think so? You think they can't see through you? They're smarter than you think."

I was a passenger in the car when the following happened. The driver was violating the speed limit. His teen-age boy was sitting with him in the front. Then the siren blew. The patrolman stopped him and pulled him to the shoulder of the outer drive in Chicago. The father looked back and said, "I'll settle this. Five bucks will take care of it." He got out five dollars and tried to bribe the policeman! Will this son respect the character of this father?

Question 7 is a great story. It isn't often that a movie moves me to emotion, but this one did at one point. I will always remember the teen-age young lad, an accomplished pianist in East Berlin. The social pressures to submit to the Communist regime are overwhelming. He is asked, along with all the students, to take the social progress questionnaire. Question 7 is, "What has been the greatest influence in your life?" Now the right an-

swers to these questions mean that he will be given
the privilege of further education. He puts the
questionnaire aside and doesn't want to answer it.
Meanwhile, the state, wanting to use him for public-
ity and propaganda purposes, urges him to go to
the Youth Festival in Berlin. His parents sincerely
object. They feel he will be compromising his con-
victions and be used by the Communists for propaganda purposes. The son chooses to neglect his parents' advice and leaves for Berlin. But before he
leaves, the father takes from the wall of the boy's
room a little plaque which was hung there the day
of his confirmation. It was the Bible text, "Be thou
faithful unto death and I will give thee a crown of
life." The next scene is Berlin. The young lad opens
his music on the piano to rehearse before the per-
formance. As he does this, out falls this paper
plaque, "Be thou faithful unto death and I will
give thee the crown of life." Just then he hears the
announcer in the auditorium broadcasting to all
East Germany over the East German radio net-
work, "Ladies and Gentlemen, you hear it said that
the Communist regime is unfair to Protestants and
to religious people. Our next contestant proves that
this is not true, for he is the son of a clergyman!"
The young Christian suddenly realizes that he is
being used. He forces an accident to his hands. In
pretended terror and pain, he runs from the room,
down the long hall, through the streets, and dashes
on through the Brandenburg Gate to freedom! The
scene shifts. News reaches the father and mother
that their son has fled to freedom rather than surrender his talents to an atheistic government. The
proud father touches the boy's desk. Then he sees
the questionnaire, "Your Social Progress." All of

the questions are blank except Question 7: "What has been the greatest influence in your life?" Behind it in bold capital letters was written: "MY FATHER."

If there is anything America needs desperately, urgently, intensely, it is fathers and mothers who rediscover and pass on to their children the Faith of the Fathers lest it be lost forever!

The Sixth Commandment:
"Thou shalt not kill"

*How did Jesus keep this commandment? Simply
by not killing, by not hating, or more positively,
by loving even those who persecuted Him? He
gave it a far profounder content. For it inspires us
to love God, to love life, to love our neighbor,
to love our enemy, and to love ourselves, too:
"Thou shalt love the Lord thy God with all thy
heart and with all thy soul and with all thy mind,
and thy neighbor as thyself."*

Chapter Six

FILL YOUR LIFE
FULL OF LOVE

We come now to the most inspiring of all the commandments.

If you are depressed by the subject of murder, suicide, and violence, and plan to skip this chapter, I hasten to call you back. This chapter may well be the most inspiring of all. Read it to its conclusion. Some days begin without sunshine. Gloomy clouds hide the golden glow. The weather is depressing. But shortly before noon the light breaks through. The needed rain has fallen. And what is more inspiring than warm rays of golden sunlight falling on pastures made green with freshly fallen rain?

See this chapter through to its conclusion. You'll be glad you did. For you will find in this section the jewel in the crown of good living.

But first we must consider the obvious argument of this commandment. For the moral implications of the law are horribly, tragically, pitifully up to date! Consider the legislature of the state of California "liberalizing" the abortion law! It is being suggested that a child that may possibly be born without arms or legs because of a drug called Thalidomine might be legitimately murdered before birth. Need we mention that over 12,000 murders were committed in America last year? This does not take into account suicides, an undetected number of abortions, a shocking number of reckless deaths needlessly committed by careless people on the highway, and senseless slaughter on the battlefield. All these "murders" remind us that this commandment is fearfully relevant.

I

To begin our discussion, let us understand that the traditional translation "Thou shalt not kill" could leave a wrong impression. Certainly God does not condemn all killing. It would then be a sin to kill a weed, or a fish, or a snake, or a chicken.

What the commandment says, of course, is that thou shalt not commit murder. Extermination of life is not outlawed. This would be unrealistic, to say the least. For plant life must be killed to sustain animal life. All humans live by eating food that was once living matter. This command does not mean that life is never to be exterminated. It *does* mean that unjustified killing is and always will be wrong in the sight of Almighty God.

But what is unjustified killing? The sacred Scriptures set forth this principle: that killing is justified if it is necessary to preserve life. Frequently, the decision is not whether we shall kill but rather who or what shall die. For instance, shall it be the germs that kill people, or shall it be the people themselves? We cannot agree with those who contend that all killing is wrong. There are people who will not kill a mouse. They have a sentimental opinion that all life is sacred, an emotional judgment that will not stand up in logic or in life. We kill rodents because we value the life of a man more than the life of a rat. And if I refuse to kill when killing would preserve life, that makes me an indirect accomplice to the crime. If a madman with a knife comes into my home to stab my wife and children sleeping in bed and I neglect to stop him on principles of "non-violence," I become a partner to the murderer. Obviously, then, this commandment does not mean that we are not permitted to kill. It does mean that unjustified killing is wrong. Killing is justified when it contributes to the preservation of human life.

Therefore the Christian Church has traditionally and historically never been pacifistic. That is, the Christian Church has always been opposed to war or to violent, aggressive action. But the Christian Church, historically, has never opposed self-defense; and many are the great saints who have given their lives in defense of freedom, faith, and family, spilling blood to preserve life. If any country should ever attack our nation, Christians can, in good conscience, go to the battle and kill the enemy, if necessary, to preserve their lives and homes. It was Elton Trueblood, the Quaker, who pointed out that more often than not, the choice is not whether we shall kill, but who shall be permitted the privilege of continuing to live![1]

II

There may be differences of opinion on what constitutes unjustified killing, but let's not waste time discussing the obvious. We all know that homicide is a sin. Only an amoral Communist would argue this point.

Perhaps we should be more concerned about parents who train their children "never to walk away from a fight but learn to grow up to defend themselves." More than one child trained on this supposedly noble principle later became guilty of manslaughter. He accidently struck his opponent "too hard." I for one am training my son that the safest, wisest, and oftentimes most courageous form of self-defense is a respectable retreat. "Don't waste your energy, your time, or your reputation on the punk who wants to fight," was the way one juvenile judge wisely worded it. The Christian parent will cultivate in his son such a sense of personal worth that fighting will naturally be considered beneath his dignity.

If homicide is murder, so is suicide. No man has a moral right to kill himself. Suicide is the murder of the self. Perhaps the Church has been too gentle at this point. We do not want to hurt the relatives

[1] Elton Trueblood in *Foundations of Reconstruction* (Harper).

of a suicide victim any more than they have been hurt already. So we courteously and intentionally neglect to point out what God says on this subject: "No murderer . . . shall enter into the kingdom of heaven." We must understand that God made every human being with an innate will to live. When life becomes extremely frustrating, depressing, or oppressive, sometimes the desire to die rises to the surface of the conscious mind. The demonic idea may knock at the door but we do not need to let it enter in and entertain it. Like it or not, the "fear of hell" has been the final restraint to halt many a would-be self-murderer. Should we preach this more often?

And our sophisticated space-age generation has dared to challenge the classic laws on abortion to force us into a discussion on this unpleasant subject. Every life deserves the chance to be born. In rare cases abortion is judged moral if absolutely necessary to preserve the life of a mother. (This is another instance of determining who would be given the privilege of continuing to live.) But to dare to attack the life of an unborn infant, and kill a defenseless child in the womb, on the theory that the infant might be born disfigured is murder before birth! Even a limbless child deserves the opportunity to prove that life without the usual limbs can be extraordinarily productive and creative. Are there not many examples in history that the handicapped are often motivated toward greater creativity? If it is right to abort the life of an unborn child that lies without arms or legs in a mother's womb, then it is also perfectly right to go into our veteran hospitals and liquidate, in the name of "mercy," the tragically wounded and limbless veterans. Does anyone want

to start a crusade? The human race would indeed
have been robbed of some of its most inspiring and
constructive citizens if every child born handicapped, or born out of rape or incest, was murdered
before birth. Every child, no matter how conceived,
by virtue of the fact that God has permitted this
life in a womb, deserves the opportunity and the
chance to be born and to prove his inherent worth.

But why is murder wrong? There is a division of
reasoning on this question. The dialectical materi-
alist says that it is wrong to kill a human life because by so doing you may eliminate a potentially
useful tool from society. Pragmatism is merciless.
To be specific, Communism declares that anyone
who is no longer useful to the state becomes
thereby a liability. Therefore, it reasons, it is a
contribution to the community at large if this dis-
eased person is no longer kept as an expense account to the state.

The core of the argument is our concept of man.
Dialectical materialism argues that man is nothing
more than a glorified thinking machine, not made
of metal, but of flesh and bone. Instead of running
on gas or electric or atomic energy, this machine
runs on bread and water. If man is nothing more
than a glorified machine, then indeed the state, like
an efficient factory, does the right thing when it
takes a rundown or a worn-out machine that would
be too costly to repair and discards it and replaces
it with good, up-to-date equipment.

From the standpoint of honest, consistent logic,
there is only one reason why it is wrong to extermi-
nate human life, and that argument is the existence
of God. Every human being is made in the image
of God. Every human being bears within his physi-

cal body an immortal soul. Every human being, no matter how sick, how inert, how old or how deformed he may be, has within him a spark of the eternal God. Man is not just a brilliant animal, a glorified thinking machine made of flesh and blood and bones, but he is a spirit that lives in a human body. Man is an eternal soul, a spiritual essence that thrives and grows in a body made of flesh and blood. But the real man is a soul. When we look at the remains in the casket, we are not looking at the person. We only see the empty house in which the person lived. Oliver Wendell Holmes was nearly ninety, and sick and tired, when somebody came to him and said, "How's Oliver Wendell Holmes?" He answered briskly, "Well, Oliver Wendell Holmes, Sir, has never been better, but this old house in which he lives is getting kind of run down. The shingles are coming off the roof and the timbers are getting a little weak. Yes, the old house in which Oliver Wendell Holmes lives is getting kind of run down, but, thank you, Sir, Oliver Wendell Holmes has never been better."

III

What is really needed is a revival of sensitivity. It is not enough for us not to murder. It not enough not to hate. Before there can be brotherhood, or love, there must be sensitivity to human suffering and grief. There is evidence that our modern generation is becoming insensitive to the feelings of our fellow men.

What is happening to us anyway? Does the death of a fellow human being no longer hurt and haunt us? At breakfast we read the headlines:

"Airplane Crashes in Idlewild, New York. 93 People Killed!" "Isn't that too bad," we say, and we lay the paper down with the calloused comment, "Pass the jelly, please." What is happening to us? I remember that years ago when there was a funeral procession coming down the road, the cars would all pull to the side and stop in a gesture of respect. Not today. Cars roar right on. What is happening to us? There are literally millions of people in our world that are living on the very edge of starvation. And we don't really care.

Christ declares that we must be sensitive to human need. "I was in hunger," he said, "and you gave me no meat. I was thirsty, and you gave me no drink; naked and you clothed me not." When we shall ask Him, "Lord, when did we do that to you?" His reply will burn like a hot sear into our conscience: "Inasmuch as you did it not unto the least of these, my brethren, you did it not unto me."

If there is a revival of sensitivity, perhaps we will see a rebirth of compassion; when we begin to be deeply disturbed and disquieted on account of human beings that are dying lonely deaths, perhaps we will really begin to care. To care is to be concerned, and concern is the first stir of compassion. And if there is compassion, men may still disagree but they will not be mean. We may still have to fight for the right, but we will not be driven by hate. A rebirth of compassion may not completely eliminate war. Sinful nations, led by sinful men, may still attempt to conquer other nations by the sword. And to preserve our lives, we may have to shoulder arms. But then there will be no torture of the enemy. Into a world filled with hate and resentment and unholy wrath, came a quiet Man who restated this timeless commandment "Thou shalt not kill": "Whoever hates his brother without a cause has committed murder in his heart already."

IV

Now, where are we? Where has this discussion led us? If you have been to our national caves, you have had the experience of entering the earth through a dark, depressing tunnel. It twists and bends deeper into the ground and becomes a narrow crevice barely large enough for a human being to squeeze through. Then, suddenly, it opens into a colossal, cavernous hollow in the depths of the earth, large enough to hold a cathedral—awesome not only by its size, but also by its stunning beauty. Sparkling stalactites and shimmering stalagmites, like marble statues and glistening chandeliers, adorn this underground cathedral of nature.

So the study of this normally morbid commandment, through the leading of Christ, has brought us to a colossal new concept, as inspiring as any cathedral, and this ancient law becomes a command to love. How did Jesus keep this commandment? Simply by not killing, by not hating, or more positively, by loving even those who persecuted Him? He gave it a far profounder content. For it inspires us to love God, to love life, to love our neighbor, to love our enemy, and to love ourselves, too: "Thou shalt love the Lord thy God with all thy heart and with all thy soul and with all thy mind, and thy neighbour as thyself."

No wonder, then, that we can confidently claim

that this command, rightly understood, shows us
God's way to the Good Life. For the person who
falls in love with life finds that living can be an inspiring experience. It is so much fun living with a
heart full of love for others! How do you go about
it? Can you change your nature? Do you tend to be
easily irritated, quickly upset by people and situations? Can you become a more loving person?

Let us be honest. *You* can't change a person's
basic nature. But Jesus Christ can! I have seen the
most unlikable persons become the most pleasant
and lovable people once Christ came into their life!

I am thinking of a man who claimed to be a
near-atheist. He was not only arrogant, he was
rude. Even this description is extremely charitable.
It is not immoderate to say that he was blatantly
offensive, using abusive language to my wife and
myself. He had no use whatever for the church and
resented bitterly the fact that his wife went there.
Today that man (no, not that same man, he is a
new creation—a truly different person) may be seen
every Sunday morning in the Garden Grove Community Church.

What changed him? The answer is simple—love
changed him; Christ changed him. "If any man be
in Christ he is a new creature." Christ literally
changed him into a completely new person. He is
full of love for life, for people, for God, and in a
very fine sense he loves and respects himself, too!

How do you begin to be a new creature? Many
people have found it works by going to church.
And if you can't wait until Sunday, you can begin
right now, wherever you are, with this simple treatment.

1. Take the telephone off the hook.

2 Close the door and lock it.

3. Get down on your knees. (Get comfortable. If you want to use a pillow under your knees, do so.)

4. Be prepared to ignore any interruption.

5. Repeat—out loud (this is important)—at least ten times this life-transforming prayer: "Jesus Christ, come into my life. Jesus Christ, come into my life."

6. After praying this prayer ten times, repeat— out loud—this affirmation: "I love Christ. I love God. I love people. I love myself. I love . . . (here, say out loud the name of any person who has offended you. Hard? Of course! No one said that this "treatment" was easy. But I guarantee that it will work! Love—or quit! Love or let your soul get sicker and sicker until you are forever lost in your own selfish misery. Now say it . . . "I love my enemy, too!").

The Seventh Commandment:
"Thou shalt not commit adultery"

Adultery was the ruin of Rome. Adultery spoiled the splendor of Greece. And history may prove that adultery brought low the once proud and mighty United States of America—unless our nation rapidly reverses the sex trend of today. For the seventh commandment is the voice of God. Its truth stands like a colossal granite rock rising out of the sea. On its immovable shores immoral nations, like reckless ships, break apart and sink into oblivion.

Chapter Seven

SEX CAN BE
BEAUTIFUL

For two weeks Allen Gordon was a living bomb! It happened in the Battle of the Coral Seas in November of 1942. Allan was on the upper deck of a "tin can"—an American destroyer—when a Japanese fighter plane strafed the deck and shot a 20-millimeter shell filled with a live explosive charge into the young American sailor's chest, through his stomach, where it lodged, silently but alive, in his right hip. A bold warning sign was wrapped around his wrist that said, "Caution—Live

20-Millimeter Slug!" The five-inch-long shell carried an explosive charge so sensitive that later in tests it effectively exploded upon being fired through tissue paper!

Perhaps you remember the rest of the story as it was seen by millions of Americans on the television show, "Navy Log." Shortly before Allan's parents joined our church in Garden Grove, they retold the story to me. Carefully, cautiously, the wounded lad was placed into a swinging cot, transported by cable over rough waters to a hospital ship that was lying by to pick up the dangerous cargo. And so the boy with the live bomb in the hip was brought to New Caledonia where two weeks later an operation was successfully performed.

Now there are millions of people who are walking the streets in neatly tailored clothes that carefully disguise the fact that they harbor in their bodies living bombs—and that potentially explosive charge is sex! When God made man, He saturated the human being with two powerful appetites, (1) hunger—that man might eat and live, (2) sex—that man might reproduce and replace himself. Now the first man and woman satisfied these native appetites with legitimate enjoyment and respectable restraint until their souls became infected with a spiritual sickness called sin. And this fall of man corrupted a divinely created drive into a dangerous urge. Love changed to lust. Sex became a living bomb in the human body. And this intimate realm of human experience has continued to be a source of human problems ever since. Let us be frank and honest. All normal human beings have inherited a sex urge which, if unrestrained by conscience or law, will explode and destroy the soul of man. To protect His children then from such moral disaster, God established a divine law. It is the seventh of the Ten Commandments: "Thou shalt not commit adultery." Hear it. Honor it. Heed it. Hold to it. This is God's answer to the sex question. It is a milestone on God's way to the Good Life.

It is high time that we seek God's wisdom on how to deal with the sex problem.

There are, as I understand it, really three answers to the sex question.

I

Repress it is one suggested solution to the problem. To make sure and certain that the bomb will not explode, bury it deep! To make sure that the river will not overflow, build a dam and stop the flow of the water.

Now this may work for some people. But more often than not the dammed river only builds up pressure until the dike bursts!

I hasten to point out that there is a difference between repression and restraint. Restraint is channeling the water in a constructive and controlled manner, with floodgates to let water flow into irrigating canals. Repression is throwing a dam across the stream and commanding the water to stop flowing.

Repression hardly seems the best solution for the average person. This may work for the few. For the many it would be not only unrealistic but most undesirable. After all, God does want the human race to propagate itself.

But repression of sex is certainly not the prob-

lem in our country today! No one is leading a
crusade to outlaw sex.

II

Release it is the other extreme. This more likely
portrays the mood of our day: Yield to your instincts. Let the water flow and find its natural
course. Don't warp your personality by restraining
yourself. Enjoy your freedom. Don't let anyone
censor your morals. Get up to date. Live by the
"new morality." Be "liberated" from the old Victo-
rian, puritanical morality and live your life to the
full. So sound the clamoring voices of the modern
generation that would be delivered from the old
seventh commandment.

Let us take a look at what is happening in our
country today.

Here we have a respected college professor who
writes an article in a national monthly magazine,
openly arguing that having premarital sexual relations is definitely advisable to determine a couple's
compatibility before the marriage is officially contracted. He poses this as a bright, new, progressive
idea—the morality of tomorrow. A new idea? Ab-
surd! It is a pitifully primitive and pagan idea!

We further have a distinguished professor of so-
ciology who suggests that our concept of the
family is woefully outdated; that we must somehow in this space age manage to free ourselves
from the timeworn restrictions of our individual
sexual activities. We are told that even our laws
against homosexuality really are terribly unscien-
tific, etc., etc. And under the aura of a university
atmosphere the dignified professor sounds so ad-

vanced in his thinking. But wait a minute. Take a good look at this "new morality" and you will find that this is only the old law of the jungle, rewritten for men in gray flannel suits driving sleek cars down concrete superhighways!

Here is another sign of the times. In an American high school, an English teacher assigned his class to study contemporary plays which had homosexuality as the basic plot. When a parent objected, the school officials corrected the situation since the plays were not on the "approved list." Whereupon the arrogant professor stormed indignantly into the classroom and without attempting to hide his anger wrote on the blackboard the new assignment—an essay on the subject, "Should literary masterpieces be censored?" How revolting! We can only conclude that some literary critics have debased the standards that mark a masterpiece! We must admit that not a few of our widely read novels are masterpieces of garbage and immorality! Let us be reasonable. Even the human body is a masterpiece of divine creation, but its display must obviously be censored and controlled.

In another city, a minister, a lawyer, and an educator foolishly sided together to oppose Christian citizens who wanted to rule out the sale of pornographic magazines in community drugstores and supermarkets. Respectable professional citizens of the community were used to protect the peddlers of paper prostitution. In their sincere but misguided thinking they argued that to suppress pornographic literature would be a violation of the freedom of the press. What dangerous extremism!

Reckless liberals and irresponsible progressives would, under the banner of human freedom, change our liberties into license. When liberty becomes the license to be licentious, society is in grave danger of self-destruction. We have too many academic fools who object to laws against promiscuous sexual activity on the grounds that these laws restrict human freedom. Well, of course, there ought to be a law against sin! God knows that man's nature is too potentially sinful to be permitted total liberty. Already Cicero said in ancient Rome: "Liberty without law will result in anarchy."

We must not, we cannot, permit a moral culture painstakingly shaped by generations of restraint and discipline to be prostituted by irresponsible intellectuals who advocate a neopaganism. America, take a fresh look at the fall of Rome and Greece and Corinth! And remember the wise words that "who will not learn the lessons of history is doomed to repeat them."

Adultery was the ruin of Rome. Adultery spoiled the splendor of Greece. And history may prove that adultery brought low the once proud and mighty United States of America—unless our nation rapidly reverses the sex trend of today. For the seventh commandment is the voice of God. Its truth stands like a colossal granite rock rising out of the sea. On its immovable shores immoral nations, like reckless ships, break apart and sink into oblivion. Release the urge? Let your instinct have its natural flow and fling? This is the answer of the jungle to the sex problem.

It is high time that we in America re-examine the basis of morality and understand:

1. That morality is not based on nature. Because some act is natural, that does not make the act necessarily right. Animal ethics is based on

natural instinct. Man, made in the image of God, bases his morality on the law of God, not on the law of nature. It may be natural for a man to want more than one woman. This does not make it moral or right. It is also natural for a man to strike out and hit his fellow man when there is a clash of interest or opinion, but this does not mean that it is right.

2. That morality is not based on personal wants, desires, or pleasures. Because I want to do something does not mean that this is right, or moral, or ethical, or good. In fact, an immoral man is someone who always does what he wants to do without considering whether or not it is the right thing to do. The average unregenerate man might enjoy the pleasures of lust, but this does not mean that lust is right.

3. That morality is not based on community standards. Because everyone is doing a certain thing, that does not make it right. Eight out of ten families on your block may never worship God, but this does not mean that they are right. How often I hear the feeble reason as a supposed moral justification, "Well, everyone else is doing it." Even your own conduct is not the basis of morality. Because you have done something, that does not mean that it is right. To illustrate, a man may be morally opposed to stealing, until in a weak moment he takes something. From that point on he may tend to say that stealing is not *always* wrong. I know a man who was opposed to divorces. He subsequently fell in love with another woman. Now suddenly he is not opposed to divorces. For a moral code and standard, we must have the courage to look beyond our own conduct and beyond the conduct of the

people of our community to the Word of God. And we must stand in that Divine light to receive the word on what is right and what is wrong.

4. That morality cannot be rationalized. A man sat in my study and told me about his troubles and failures. I could not refrain from telling him that his problems were largely of his own making. He was his own worst enemy. He had too often behaved very foolishly. Then he turned to me and said, "Well, Reverend, if you had had the kind of a life I had, and if you had been raised in the home that I was raised in, you would understand why I am the way I am. I have talked to psychologists and I know why I am the way I am. It was because of my childhood." He was able to explain "why" he did it and this he considered sufficient reason to vindicate his conduct. But the "why" does not always justify. You cannot rationalize morality. To have certain reasons for your conduct does not mean it is right. If a little boy is neglected by his parents and steals money to buy himself a pair of shoes, does this make stealing right? Of course not.

The foundation of morality, then, is the Word of God. An act is right or wrong depending on the will of God expressed in that Word. Deny the existence of God and you have no firm, solid, authoritative basis for morality.

III

God's Word on the question of sex is not to repress it, nor to release it, but to *redeem it.* Don't bury the bomb. Don't blast the bomb. But delicately disarm the bomb and use the potentially explosive power creatively. Don't try to dam the river without floodgates. Channel the water into controlled canals that can irrigate dry deserts and transform useless sand into fruitful farmlands.

The sex drive generates great energy in the human personality. This energy must be redeemed, harnessed, channeled, sublimated. Then it will be a creative force.

The nations that have respected the Ten Commandments have created a great culture called Western civilization. In this grand and glorious culture, the sex drive is sublimated through monogamous marriage. One husband and one wife are united till death ends the union.

So the sex urge is channeled to create the most beautiful of all institutions: the family. And in this setting, man creates his most beautiful masterpiece: a baby.

For the most beautiful picture in the world is not a snowcapped mountain, or a gorgeous sunset, or even the fresh burst of a new flower. The most beautiful picture in the world is the picture of a husband and a wife with their little children gathered in their arms. A strong family, united in love, united in faith, united in loyalty to each other and proud of each other is the picture of God's majestic and magnificent answer to the sex question. This is the sex drive sublimated and redeemed.

And now you can see why adultery is wrong, terribly wrong! It ruins the picture. It spoils the whole lovely scene. It wrecks the beautiful portrait like a vandal with a knife who slashes a beautiful masterpiece in an art gallery.

I don't have to tell you what adultery is. You know. It is sharing sex outside of the bonds of holy matrimony. Yes and often it is divorce (Matt. 5:27-32). We can agree that there are times when a divorce is justified. Even Jesus said that. But even when a divorce is justified, it is still a mistake, for it still spoils forever what should have been a beautiful picture. But if it has happened to you and it is too late to correct, then seek God's pardon for your mistake and with God's guidance build a happy future.

And what can we say to those who in the mystery of Divine Providence are not permitted the privilege of marriage? Here, also, the sex energies must be redeemed and sublimated. How? These physical energies can be satisfied in community-service projects, hobbies, recreations, advanced studies, or in the discovery and development of new talents. The truth is that the history of charitable organizations shows that some of our greatest public servants have been celibates by chance or by choice.

"How can you keep clean?" you ask. How can you win against the temptation to commit adultery? There are many ways to victory, but best of all, get Jesus Christ into your heart and life. If a spark of fire balls on the cement sidewalk, nothing happens. But when a spark of fire falls into a gasoline tank there is an explosion. The temptation to commit adultery falls on the man who has Christ in his heart like a spark falling on water, or concrete; but when the spark of temptation falls on the heart of a man who does not have God in his life, it is like a spark of fire falling on a powder keg and the living bomb explodes!

The Eighth Commandment:
"Thou shalt not steal"

It takes brave men to face the moral implications of this commandment. For we arrive at a point where we see that what this law contains is the God-ordained foundation of man's rights and man's responsibilities. It is no sin to be a capitalist, but it is a sin to be selfish. It is no sin to be wealthy, but it is a sin to be greedy. It is no sin to work for profit, but it is a sin to exploit the unfortunate.

Chapter Eight

KNOW YOUR RIGHTS
AND RESPONSIBILITIES

Obeying this commandment calls for brave men.
For it takes courage to explore the central truths
in this great lesson in living. Do we dare to hear
the message of this sacred sentence?

I suppose you have not been guilty of theft, but
over eleven billion dollars were stolen outright in
America last year. Thievery and embezzlement are
big business in our land!

In addition, over three billion dollars is spent an-
nually in that crime called gambling. America, a

country built on the Ten Commandments, has seen fit to outlaw uncontrolled gambling. And rightly so.

Recently a friend said to me: "But, Reverend, I don't see why I shouldn't gamble. After all, I enjoy it and I just spend a little money at it." "There are two things wrong with your thinking," I pointed out. "In the first place, the moral person doesn't ask, 'Do I enjoy it?' But rather, 'Is it right?' The second mistake in your reasoning is the 'little bit' argument. It is as wrong to steal a quarter as it is to steal a dollar. I am reminded of the foolish doctor who told the unmarried expectant mother: 'Don't worry, you are only a little bit pregnant.' " We must refrain from gambling and theft because they aim at getting another person's property without working for it. And this is a solid, sound, stable principle. And we are governed by principles—not pleasures!

There is ample evidence that America is in a real moral depression. And the results of a moral depression are more tragic than those of an economic depression. Have we forgotten payola already? or the TV scandals? Perhaps someone can tell me how much money was stolen in America last year by corporations that declared bankruptcy while the clever business heads protected their personal wealth through corporation laws! God only knows the money that has been stolen by padded expense accounts, inflated bills, exaggerated charges, false statements of time spent on jobs, etc.

Yes, America is sick! Do we intend to pay that loan back? Neglected bills, borrowing without repaying, taking and not giving back as we had promised are part of the problem. And how about taking charity that we do not need? Public relief has become a major source of immorality in our land today. I am not opposed to deserved charity, properly administered. I would not be a Christian if I did not have a heart. But I remember, too, that Wanamaker, that great philanthropist, was once asked, "What was the hardest job you faced in your life?" To which he answered, "How to give away money without doing more harm than good!" Wise men see that welfare can easily corrupt.

The real question at this point is: Is it right to accept charity when we do not need it? Is it right to take a handout from my church, my county, my country, if I can pay my own way? I declare that the moral principle implied in this commandment is violated by the man who takes charity when he could get along without it. I watched a man ahead of me in a supermarket buy two six-packs of beer and three cartons of cigarettes, and pay for these items with a local welfare check! I object to that. I object to the unemployed woman's complaining because she had received an offer to go back to work. "I'll only earn $88 a week for five day's work," she said, "when I can get almost half that much for staying home!" What is happening to America?

Someone told me that the government is considering paying the bill for vaccinating every child in America. Does that mean that the government will tax some corporation, private business, or some personal citizen's private wealth to give my child free vaccine? Well, I can afford to pay for my own child's vaccine. Let us get back to the great old idea of paying our own bills. And if we can't, we can apply for relief. But let us understand that to take charity when we can pay our own way destroys the soul and the spirit and the character of a man.

It might not hurt America to re-examine the financial structure of our public school system. My children are not getting free medical care and free dental care, but they are getting free education. Frankly, I could afford to pay their educational expenses. But the government pays the bill. My taxes do not begin to cover the actual expenses of my child's education. Should the government send the bill for my child's education in the form of a tax bill to my neighbor who may happen to have a very profitable factory? Should I let industry pay my child's way? Perhaps this is the expedient way of underwriting public education. But I wonder if it is the best way. Is it the right way? Has America now reached a level of prosperity where every family might be challenged to pay the bill for his child's education exactly like he pays for his child's medical or dental bill? Would parents perhaps take greater interest in their child's education if they had to pay for it themselves? If I can afford to have a stereophonic hi-fi, all of the modern conveniences, and drive a late-model car, and if I can afford to pay for the education of my child, is it right for me to allow half of his educational, or medical, or dental expenses be paid—forcibly through taxation—by someone who happens to have a profitable business?

Yes, it takes brave men to face the moral implications of this commandment. For we arrive at a point where we see that what this law contains is the God-ordained foundation of man's *rights* and man's *responsibilities*. If you really want to live

the good life, find out what your God-given rights
are!

I

"Thou shalt not steal" guarantees to every individual the right to own property. Communism is
the state violating the eighth commandment.
Western civilization has seen in the eighth commandment a God-ordained right which most naturally expressed itself in an economic philosophy
called capitalism. For the Christian saw that every
man has a right to own a house, a plot of ground, a
business, or a bank account.

Too, you have a God-ordained right to be
wealthy. You are a steward of the good, the gold,
the gifts, that God has allowed to come into your
hands. Having riches is no sin. Wealth is no crime.
Christ did not praise poverty. The profit motive is
not necessarily unchristian!

So you have a God-given right to be a capitalist.
No wonder that the Christian and Jewish countries
have given rise to the capitalistic system! We have
been taught that it is wrong to take help from the
state if we can pay our own way. No wonder the
Christian religion has not been historically associ-
ated with socialism. We have been taught it is a sin
to steal from the rich and give to the poor. No
wonder the Christian Church has been opposed to
Communism.

In the final analysis this means that you have
the right to be free. To have the right to own property, to accumulate wealth, to be a capitalist,
means ultimately the right to be free. For no man
is really free unless he is financially independent.
My father is financially independent; he is a

farmer. He lives from the income from his capital investment. And he has a freedom of speech which many an employed person does not have. He can speak out on controversial issues without having to be afraid that his income will suffer. He is free. Now, many of us will not achieve financial independence. But the right to become financially independent is a right guaranteed to every man who lives in a capitalistic country that respects free enterprise. And this is a right that finds its sure footing in the words "Thou shalt not steal."

II

But this commandment not only points to our God-ordained rights, it also reminds us of our God-ordained responsibilities. Rights always imply responsibilities. Two fundamental human responsibilities grow out of this command. The first is to work. If you want something, God declares you may not try to get it for nothing by stealing or gambling. If you want something, you must work for it. You have no right to expect the state to take care of you.

Here is a major signpost on God's way to good living: The unhappy man is the one who is not working. The unemployed, the forcibly retired, the physically handicapped have a constant battle against boredom, monotony, and that feeling of uselessness.

Self-respect, self-esteem, personal pride and self-confidence are the priceless rewards that God bestows upon the man who follows His way and works for what he wants.

Are you unhappy? How long has it been since you have done a good day's work? When a man has spent his utmost energy at a worthwhile task he feels good! How guilty we feel when we have not worked hard and long at the job. Thank God for work.

Do you feel useless and unimportant? How generous have you been in sharing your self, your talents, your substance with the less fortunate? We have a God-given right to be rich but we also have a God-given responsibility to share with those who are in need. The right and the responsibility cannot be separated from each other without damaging our whole economic system. For this reason Christian countries have at the same time produced capitalists and great philanthropists. Take stock and see the hospitals, libraries, churches, schools, colleges, medical research centers, charitable foundations, international missions with hospitals and schools, and the like, that have been produced by Christian capitalism.

It is no sin to be a capitalist, but it is a sin to be selfish. It is no sin to be wealthy, but it is a sin to be greedy. It is no sin to work for profit, but it is a sin to exploit the unfortunate.

It is our God-given responsibility to share, voluntarily, cheerfully, compassionately, with those who are in need. And in this sense, our nation has always had a Christian conscience. If a neighbor down the street suffers great financial problems and is burdened with overwhelming medical bills, the community traditionally rises to its responsibilities and helps meet the need. No man needs to starve in a Christian land.

But the welfare state is endangering this community spirit. "Let them apply for aid," the neighbors said in a certain community when a case of human tragedy occurred. "Let the government help them," was the opinion. The peril of socialism is right there where the individual shifts his responsibility to the state. And if American capitalists are not willing to share, we may well find God withdrawing our freedoms. Rights will be withdrawn where responsibilities are neglected.

Moreover, to neglect to share with those in need is a form of stealing too. God said centuries ago, "You have robbed me!" The people were shocked. It is bad enough to rob your neighbor but would a man rob God? "Wherein have we robbed thee?" they asked. And God's answer came back to jolt their greedy hearts: "In tithes and offerings" (Mal. 3:8).

God has told us again and again that He will give to man the right to own property, the energy to accumulate wealth; but we have the responsibility to return to Him who keeps our heart beating ten percent of everything He allows to come into our hand. This is tithing. He promises that if we take our right and accept our responsibility, He will bless us far beyond our imagination: "Bring ye all your tithes into the storehouse and prove me [test Me, try Me!] and see if I will not open the windows of heaven and pour you out blessings so that there shall not be room enough to receive it" (Mal. 3:10). This is God's word to men who want to be capitalists.

And before we criticize the man who takes welfare funds to buy beer and whisky and cigarettes, we must remember that there are members in the church who claim that they cannot possibly afford to tithe but who also buy beer and liquor and cigarettes. Let us be honest now—is this right?

The Ninth Commandment:
"Thou shalt not bear false witness
against thy neighbor"

Look for the good in people. You will find what you look for. When the vulture flies over the desert, he looks for nothing but a rotten carcass, because that's his meat. A hummingbird will fly over the same desert and never see the carcass, because he is looking for a flower. You will be properly proud of yourself when you go through life seeing the lovely in the unlovely, spotting the rose in the desert, pointing out the lily that grows among the thorns. Your reward will be a wonderful feeling of self-respect.

Chapter Nine

HOW TO GET PEOPLE TO HOLD YOU IN HIGH ESTEEM

Jesus Christ was crucified by words before He was killed on a cross. Follow me now to the scene of Christ's trial in the judgment hall. Jesus is the tall One, in the white robe, with the long flowing hair, the uncalloused hands, the gentle heart and the tender eyes. He is surrounded by accusers, and yet He stands alone. There is no one at His side to defend Him. There is no friend to bear good witness to Him. There are only those who bring false reports, irresponsible charges and false witness against Him. Hours later, He hangs limp under the terribly hot Palestinian sky. He is dead. And the cross, through the centuries, remains not only a beautiful symbol of God's redemptive love of men, but at the same time a gruesome and ghastly reminder of man's inhumanity against his fellow man.

While the eighth commandment was designed to protect property, the ninth commandment was given by God to protect the truth. One thing is sure: if you want people to respect you and hold you in high esteem, you will have to be careful to build a reputation of being a man who honors the truth.

I

To begin with, be careful to distinguish between facts and opinions. Today I am the minister of a beautiful million-dollar drive-in church. Several years ago we started this work in a drive-in theater. Again and again I heard a remark that went something like this: "The drive-in church is a bad invention. It creates laziness. It is most irreverent." This comment was stated as a fact. The truth is this comment was only someone's personal opinion. And it so happens that time has proven the opinion to be wrong. Many people who for legitimate reasons must remain in the privacy of their cars are able to join in worship as they cannot walk into a traditional sanctuary. Lest we unwittingly assassinate the truth, let us preface our comments with the qualifying phrase, "In my opinion."

Assassination of truth occurs when we declare as a fact an idea which in all honesty is merely our personal interpretation. Consider the minister who approaches an obviously obscure part of the Bible and declares arbitrarily, "This is what God is saying!" If this minister was truly responsible, he would in all honesty introduce his argument by saying, "It is my personal interpretation that . . . etc., etc." All too often we find out that we have misinterpreted some document, some statement, some comment, some friend's remarks, some speaker's message. It is wise for us to approach someone who has upset us by quietly asking, "Am I correct in interpreting your remark to mean . . .?" Or we might question a critic by asking him, "Do I understand you right . . .? Do you mean to say . . .?" How often we will find that we misinterpreted the point.

If we are going to honor the truth, we will be careful to distinguish between fact and impression. You have heard how some people talk: "He certainly isn't very friendly," or "He's awfully opinionated," or "She certainly is not very spiritual." We declare to be a fact what in reality is only a personal impression.

How often, after we have learned to know a person better, we discover that we had the wrong impression.

It is most irresponsible to form an impression of a person by the clothes he wears, the manner of his speech, the expression on his face, or the manner of his walk.

The man who holds his head high may give the impression of being proud. The truth is he may only have cultivated a habit of fine posture. If you must talk about a person, you should admit in all honesty that you are only relating what is your personal impression and admit that your impression may not be accurate.

And if you want to win a man's respect you will not confuse judgments with facts. "He is telling a lie," we declare. "That is a crime," we complain. "That is slander!" we shout. What we are doing is passing judgment. Our judgment may be right or it may be wrong, but let us be honest and admit, "It is my personal judgment that this man is not telling the truth." After all, more than one judge on the bench has judged amiss. That is why we have higher courts where we can appeal the judgment of a lower court.

Certainly you don't win friends by tale-bearing. Tale-bearing is passing on stories that are half true. And even though some tales may be completely true, it would be better to leave them buried, forgotten and unrepeated.

If you see a tall fellow ahead of the crowd,
Marching fearless and brave with head held
*   proud,*
And you know of a tale whose mere telling aloud
Would cause his proud head to be humbly
*   bowed,*
It's a pretty good plan to forget it!

I suppose everybody knows something bad somebody has done somewhere along the line. Forget it. Why tell somebody else about it? In the book of Proverbs, we read these words, "Where there is no wood, the fire goes out." Where there is no one to tell tales, the memory dies. I cannot resist underlining a well-circulated story here. Once there was a Catholic priest who made calls regularly in the home of a young widow. Somebody started passing a rumor. Some busybody began to be suspicious. Two ladies "put two and two together" and began to gossip. Suddenly the young widow died and the community was informed that she had been secretly sick with cancer. Only her priest knew about it. He came regularly to pray for her and to help her. But someone with a dirty mind had started talking. The two ladies who were responsible for it all came to the priest and said, "We are sorry, truly sorry. Why didn't you tell us, Father?" (A priest or a minister frequently cannot defend himself without violating somebody else's confidence.) The priest answered, "All right, if you're sorry, take this feather pillow, go to the top of the hill, and let the feathers fly where the wind will carry them." And they did. When they came back with their empty pillow case they said, "Father, we have done this. Now, will you forgive us?" The priest answered, "Not until you go out and pick up every feather and put them all back in the sack and bring it back to me." They said, "But that is impossible, Father. The winds have blown the feathers to the four corners." To which he replied, "So it is with your words."

II

Truth is not only assassinated, it is also exaggerated. There are two kinds of exaggeration. Real enthusiasm often leads to exaggeration and this is usually quite harmless.

Exaggeration is dangerous when superlatives and absolutes are used recklessly, such as "He's never on time," or "She always nags me," or "They are

completely wrong," or "They are all against me."
Now wait a minute. Think what you are saying.
You are using absolute words—never, completely,
always, all. You have never been happy in your marriage you say? Never? Careful, friend, you may be
exaggerating. You may have forgotten or you are
unable to recollect and your memory may not be
serving you correctly. Maybe you have been having
trouble and tension for only a few months.

We exaggerate by making unstudied, generalized
statements. I have sat in committees when someone proposed some wonderful positive idea. A certain plan was so exciting! Suddenly some nega-
tively inclined person would make a dangerous, irresponsible exaggeration—"Men, it will cost $5,-
000!" He uttered his unstudied opinion as if it
were a fact. And the idea might drop dead at that
point. It could very well be that if a careful up-to-
date study was made, it might be possible to carry
out the plan for $2,800.

Some years ago I was attending the Ministerial
Association in our city. Someone suggested that the
Protestant churches get together, pool their man-
power and make a door-to-door canvass of the
town, inviting every family in the city to attend
church. Immediately, one minister said, "Gentlemen, this is impossible. There are fourteen thousand homes in the city. It would take a year and
goodness knows how many people. It is a good
idea, but it simply isn't practical." Well, that end-
ed that. The originator of the idea made a few
feeble efforts to pick up new enthusiasm but without success, and the idea was dropped.

I went home from that meeting, deeply disturbed. I met with a couple of positive thinkers in

my church who believe that nothing is impossible. One of these young men said, "Let's do it. All we need is seventy people who will agree to ring two hundred doorbells in a two-week period of time!" I am proud to say that in three weeks the organization was set up, and in a two-week period of time one congregation did what was considered to be too big a job for twenty Protestant churches put together!

God only knows how many missions have never been established, how many churches have never been built, how many great projects have never been launched because of exaggerated negative comments by people who lack enough faith.

III

Furthermore, we violate truth by insinuations. The story is told of a first mate who often became inebriated on board ship. He was warned by the captain that if he became intemperate once more the offense would be recorded in the ship's log. It did happen. The captain kept his word and wrote indelibly in the ship's log: "Tuesday, March 14, First Mate Drunk." This really hurt the old sailor and he vowed to take vengeance. Two days later he slipped into the captain's quarters and wrote in the ship's log, "Thursday, March 16, Captain Sober Today."

How subtle, dangerous, and cowardly is this business of insinuation and innuendo. It is also evident in the technique of asking suggestive questions. For instance: "Do you think John has been faithful to his wife?" Or, "I wonder why he did it." Or, "Do you think he really means it?" Insinuating

questions can defame a man's character. We do it
by sarcastic name-dropping: "Oh, John!" Or,
"Haven't you met John yet? You will!" Thus simply by dropping a name in a certain tone of a
voice, we have borne false witness. And how about
silence? We insinuate a person's guilt when he is
accused in our presence and we know him to be in-
nocent but lack the courage to rise to his defense.
Our silence makes us an accomplice to the crime.
In some sophisticated circles, even a compliment
can become an insinuation. You've heard it: "Well,
I think he's improving." Or, "I think he's making
progress." Or, "Isn't it too bad that his talents
haven't been discovered yet?"

IV

Now, if we can violate this commandment by as-
sassinations, by exaggeration, by insinuation, we
also can do it by rationalization. We rationalize by
justifying our prejudices, defending our mistakes,
explaining away our shortcomings, and vindicating
our sins. The human being has great capacity to be
dishonest with himself. We will not improve our
life or our lot so long as we don't forthrightly face
up to our own personality problems.

On the other hand, there are too many people
who rationalize by underestimating themselves. If
it is a sin to bear false witness against our neighbor, it is also a sin to bear false witness against
yourself. It is popular today to cut oneself down to
almost nothing, to admit publicly all one's mistakes and shortcomings. This apparently is supposed to be a dramatic display of humility. But
don't bear false witness against yourself! Most of

you are better than you think you are. Most of you
you are loved and esteemed and respected by more
people than you know of. You just don't have
enough confidence in yourself and you don't have
enough faith in yourself. Most people like you.
You are not going to win esteem by downgrading
yourself. God made you. Don't belittle, underrate
and insult the Lord's own creation!

You will win the respect and esteem of great men
when you cultivate an appreciation, first of all, for
people. Look for the good in people. You will find
what you look for. When the vulture flies over the
desert, he finds a rotten carcass, because that's
what he is looking for. A hummingbird will fly over
the same desert and never see the carcass, because
he is looking for a flower!

You find what you look for, and "there's so
much good in the worst of us, and there's so much
bad in the best of us, that it hardly behooves any
of us to condemn anyone." You feel so good when
you look for the good in people. But you begin to
feel so mean, so critical, so negative, when you are
looking for the bad in people.

Here is a solid road to good living: Learn to love
people! Remember how happy you are when you
love people? Remember how unhappy you felt
when you were criticizing, gossiping, belittling, or
condemning another human being, made in the
image of Almighty God?

The secret of self-esteem is right here. You will
be properly proud of yourself when you go through
life seeing the lovely in the unlovely, spotting the
rose in the desert, pointing out the lily that grows
among the thorns. Is this not the clue to every inspiring life? Is this not the spirit of Jesus? He

looked at men of weakness and pointed out their possibilities, declaring: "You are the light of the world." Truly, the greatest joy in life is to discover the good in a person and then to bring that goodness out.

You will come to a point where you will even appreciate a person in spite of his shortcomings. You will not become irresponsibly tolerant of evil, but your ill-feelings will be moderated by your awareness that his apparent weakness may be hidden strength.

Is he "too easygoing"? Perhaps this is because he is so understanding. Is he "too authoritative"? Perhaps this is because he has strong leadership abilities. Is he "too officious"? Perhaps this is because he is so eager to serve.

Make a game of finding the best in others. It is real fun finding the good in the worst. Your reward will be a wonderful feeling of self-respect.

The Tenth Commandment:
"Thou shalt not covet"

The tenth commandment challenges the materialism of our day. God is saying that if you want to have a life of joy and peace, and a sense of fulfillment, you will not find this in material things. Do not, then, go out and covet your neighbor's house or his car or his hi-fi or "anything that is thy neighbour's." Listen to Jesus: Be not so concerned about things. Do not be so concerned about your house and clothes. Seek first the kingdom of God and his righteousness, and all these things shall be yours as well.

Chapter Ten

HERE'S TO A GENUINELY SATISFYING LIFE

We come now to God's tenth commandment, His summary statement, His final rule for good living.

Here we shall discover the formula for fulfillment, the secret of satisfaction, and the key to contentment.

For this commandment is aimed at the person who lives a very dissatisfied life. Do you sometimes sense that you are missing out on something but you don't quite know on what? The person who has inordinate desires and who covets his neighbor's position or property is a person who deep within himself is frustrated.

Now God wants us to live the good life. And if we positively apply these Ten Commandments to daily living, we will enjoy the good life. And if you want to know what is meant by the good life, direct your attention to Jesus Christ. This was the good life incarnate.

What was life like for Him? Take a look at His last days on earth and you will see the secret of His satisfying life. Shortly before He died He said to His apostles, "I would that my joy might be in you and that your joy might be complete" (John 15:11). The good life, then, is a life that has an inner joy.

Then hear this: "Peace I leave with you, my peace I give unto you: not as the world giveth, give I unto you. Let not your heart be troubled, neither let it be afraid" (John 14:27). The good life is a life that has a deep undercurrent of profound peace.

The last words to fall from Christ's lips, as He hung and died under the Jerusalem sky, were short and simple, but triumphant: "It is finished" (John 19:30). He had carried out His divine mission. The good life is the awareness of fulfillment. For "every man's life is a plan of God." God has a plan for you. And the good life is the deep feeling that we are fulfilling God's plan and purpose in our life.

This I submit is the good life: inner joy, deep peace, and a sense of accomplishment.

How can you have it?

The tenth commandment points out very dramatically how *not* to have it. For this commandment challenges the materialism of our day. God is saying that if you want to have a life of joy and peace, and a sense of fulfillment, you will not find this in material things. Do not, then, go out and covet your neighbor's house or his car or his hi-fi or "anything that is thy neighbour's." "Things" do not bring joy or peace or a sense of fulfillment.

Madison Avenue would have us believe that the good life is something you can buy. Purchase the right product, live in the right kind of a house, wear the right kind of clothes, belong to the proper country club, serve the right kind of whiskey, and you are supposedly living the good life!

Now, this is mockery. "Things" do not satisfy the deep inner urges of our heart. Matter cannot satisfy the spirit. To begin with, things are temporal; they rust, wear out, burn out, break, or pass out of style; and man has an incurable urge to be eternal. He has an irresistible impulse to contribute to immortality. Material things make no contribution to immortality. Subconsciously we sense this. That is why materialism leaves us with an empty feeling. *Man is born an eternal creature,* and we have a profound satisfaction when we feel that we have contributed something of lasting value. Temporal things just don't satisfy the eternal spirit within us.

Oh, there are broken-down exceptions—some things seem to survive the centuries. You can go to Egypt and see the Great Pyramid which was built 5000 years ago. This is actually not very old as far as history is concerned, but it is the oldest structure standing in the world. Things don't satisfy, for things are temporal.

Furthermore, materialism does not satisfy because it is tyrannical, and *man was born to be free!*

We all know about the tyranny of things. We find that we don't own a house—the house owns us. We are married to a mortgage. We become slaves to gadgets and garments. After we have all our "things" purchased, delivered, and installed, and have enjoyed a fleeting sense of pleasure, we find that they are still dominating, dictating, and demanding. "Press me, polish me, patch me, paint me, prune me, plaster me, repair me," they shout. So we spend the best years of our lives and the bulk of our money working for "things," until, discouraged and depressed, we discover that we have no time left to pursue life's really enjoyable avocations: visiting friends, having fun, and, yes, even going to church regularly. Thus mastered by materialism, tyrannized by things, we have no time left to do the deeds, or see the places, or visit the people, that would really give us great inner joy.

To understand the futility of the materialistic life further, we must come to see that materialism begets monotony; and boredom is one of the major obstacles to the good life. Life quickly becomes monotonous. Things rapidly bore us. That is why styles have to change periodically. There has to be the long look, the short look, the baggy look, the sacky look, or the bloated look, but there has to be a *new* look, always. So we have to re-upholster, replace, redecorate, or, at least, re-arrange the furniture. Things bore us.

We get a certain amount of excitement in shopping for it, looking for it, waiting for it to be delivered, putting it just in the right place, maybe admiring it for a day or two or three, and then suddenly, days, weeks, months pass and we haven't even been conscious of this "thing" for which we

work, slave and spend our lives. To break our boredom, then, we must get on to a new "kick"—a
new-car kick, or a new-carpet kick, even a new-cat
kick—anything! So briefly we break the boredom.
Momentarily we have mastered monotony! We
have a new interest, a new cause, a new project.

But things continue to bore us. They bore us because they are dead. They never change. They are
the same, week after week after week. That is one
of the brillliant insights of Mr. Neutra, the
architect of the beautiful sanctuary in which I
preach every Sunday morning. This great architect
discovered that even buildings, like things, become
boring to people because they don't change. You
can't redecorate it every week. You can't re-arrange the furniture every week. But Mr. Neutra
discovered that there are some things that always
change—the sky, the grass, the trees, and water.
One day the water is perfectly placid and calm and
the next day it will be shivering with ripples. "Build
the building," Mr. Neutra reasoned, "so that it is
surrounded by something that will always change,
and you won't get tired of it." So, our church is
surrounded by trees, flowers, grass and sky, and
beautiful pools of water.

Yes, things bore us because things are dead.
They do not talk, or laugh, or love. And *man was
born for fellowship*. We are not happy unless we
have friends. Even an argument is better than
loneliness. No man is happy with things because
they don't satisfy his natural hunger for compan-
ionship.

Now there are exceptions, of course. Some
"things" really seem to satisfy us. But these are the
"objects of affection." It may be a work of art that

satisfies us because it speaks of some man's creative talent. It may be a sentimental something which satisfies because it re-awakens happy memories and for a moment is a substitute for the real person. Think of some of the things that satisfy: little children's shoes, grandfather's Bible, mother's favorite piece of jewelry, a treasured gift from your true love. But we must understand that the only reason these things seem to satisfy is because we identify them with some person we love, or some experience that was beautiful.

Now we are beginning to see what really satisfies in life. *Love* is the fulfillment of life. For man is born to love. See how brilliant is the insight of Christ into the human heart when He says, "Thou shalt love the Lord thy God with all thy heart and with all thy soul and with all thy mind. This is the first and great commandment. And the second is like unto it—thou shalt love thy neighbour as thyself."

This is why no person will really feel whole and complete until he has met God, for "God is love" (I John 4:8).

Once Christ came to visit the home of Mary and Martha. Martha was so busy in the kitchen with the dishes and the food and the house and the clothes that she thought she had no time to come out to talk to Jesus. She was so concerned about things that she had no time for people, so concerned about her house that she had no time for God. So Jesus said, "O, Martha, you are so concerned about so many things, so many things. And only one thing is really needed."

And that is God!

Christ makes this point very clear in the Sermon

on the Mount: "Blessed are they that hunger and thirst after righteousness, for they shall be satisfied" (Matt. 5:6).

There you have it—the formula for fulfillment, the key to contentment, the secret of satisfaction.

Do you understand? I hope so. Listen to Jesus: Be not so concerned about things. Do not be so concerned about your house and your clothes. Consider the lilies of the field, how they grow. They toil not, neither do they spin, and yet I say unto you that even Solomon in all his glory was not arrayed like one of these. Seek first the kingdom of God and his righteousness, and all these things will come (Matt. 6:27-33).

The feeling of fulfillment is in finding faith. Most of you understand and know that. You have felt the throb of God in your heart. You have prayed to Him and felt His presence. And these great spiritual experiences are real. No wonder they satisfy.

But the rest of you—do you want a satisfying life, a life without that hollow feeling, that empty feeling, that purposeless kind of an existence that you sometimes sense? Then the answer is: God, and nothing else—nothing else! And you will find God, when you come to Jesus Christ. So often people have said to me, "Well, if there is a God, why haven't we seen Him? If there is a God, why hasn't He given us an opportunity to look at Him?" I have pointed out that He has done this once, and only once. Why once? "Why has God not reincarnated Himself to each generation?" someone once asked me. The answer is obvious—once was enough. Once He has drawn the curtain and lifted the veil and given us a glimpse of what He is really like by coming down to our level.

King James of Scotland used to dress in the clothes of a peasant from time to time and then walk through the villages and the countryside. Nobody knew that this was the king. He did this in order that he might find out how the people were thinking, what their agonies were, what their heartaches and their problems amounted to. He was a king getting down to the people's level.

I believe that Jesus Christ was God visiting the world.

Why do I believe that Jesus was the Christ? Because He claimed to be God, and no intelligent man has ever called Jesus Christ a liar.

Let us listen to His own testimony. He says, "I am the light of the world." What a statement! What a claim! If He is not telling the truth then He is making a most boastful claim, is He not?

Listen to Him when He says, "I am the vine, you are the branches. Except you abide in me, you can do nothing." Listen to Him when He says, "The son of man has power to forgive sins." What authority! What a divine declaration of His preeminent position!

And listen to Him as He bears witness before Caiaphas, the high priest. He is being tried, as you know, for blasphemy before the Jewish court. He is accused of calling Himself God. They ask Him to recant. They urge Him to retract His statement. They almost beg Him to say that He was wrong, or that they had misinterpreted or misunderstood Him, and that He really didn't mean to give this impression. Would He correct the false impression now? Would He enlighten the people who had been so ignorant as to think that He was claiming divine messiahship? He would not. Why not? Because He could not. He could not tell a lie. As St. John sums it up: "God so loved the world that he gave his only begotten Son, that whosoever believeth in him should not perish, but have everlasting life."

The greatest news in the world is that God has visited this earth. He has walked this planet. He has made His great pronouncements. He has uttered His voice. He has spoken His mind. He has declared His will. H∍ has revealed His heart.

It is Jesus who reveals to the human race that God is "the eye that never closes, the ear that is never shut, the mind that never stops thinking, the heart that never grows cold."

God would be only a vague idea, an irresponsible product of someone's imagination, an unreliable exercise of human philosophizing, if it were not for Jesus Christ. Interpret Jesus as you wish, but one fact emerges clearly—God becomes real to those who draw close to Christ. So listen to Him when He says: "Come unto me, all you who labor and are heavy-laden. Come unto me, and I will give you rest." Come unto me, you with the empty, hollow lives. And when you come, don't intellectualize, analyze or diagnose Him. Simply bow; simply believe; simply bend your knee. Here's to a good life for you!

ABOUT THE AUTHOR

ROBERT H. SCHULLER is founder and senior minister of the famed Crystal Cathedral in Garden Grove, California. His telecast, "The Hour of Power" is one of the most widely viewed programs in television history. The author of fifteen books, Dr. Schuller has received many awards and several honorary degrees. His bestselling Bantam titles are *Tough Times Never Last, But Tough People Do, Tough-Minded Faith for Tender-Hearted People, Reach Out for New Life* and *Positive Prayers for Power-Filled Living.*